Name ______________________________

Copy the sample letters.

A A B B C C D D

E E F F G G H H

I I J J K K L L

M M N N O O P P

Q Q R R S S T T

U U V V W W

X X Y Y Z Z

Name ______________________________

Say the name of each letter as you trace it.

A B C D

E F G H I J

K L

M N O

P Q R S T U

V W X Y Z

Name ______________________________

Look at each box.
Draw a line from each letter
to the matching letter.

A	B	I	L
B	D	J	I
C	A	K	J
D	C	L	K
E	F	M	O
F	H	N	P
G	E	O	M
H	G	P	N

Name ______________________________

Look at each box.
Draw a line from each letter to the matching letter.

Q	R	U	V
R	T	V	U
S	Q	W	X
T	S	X	W

Y	Z	U	V
Z	Q	V	R
Q	Y	W	W
Z	Z	R	U

Name ______________________________

Draw a line to the right little sister.

Name ______________________________

Color the alligator and write the number of A's in the box.

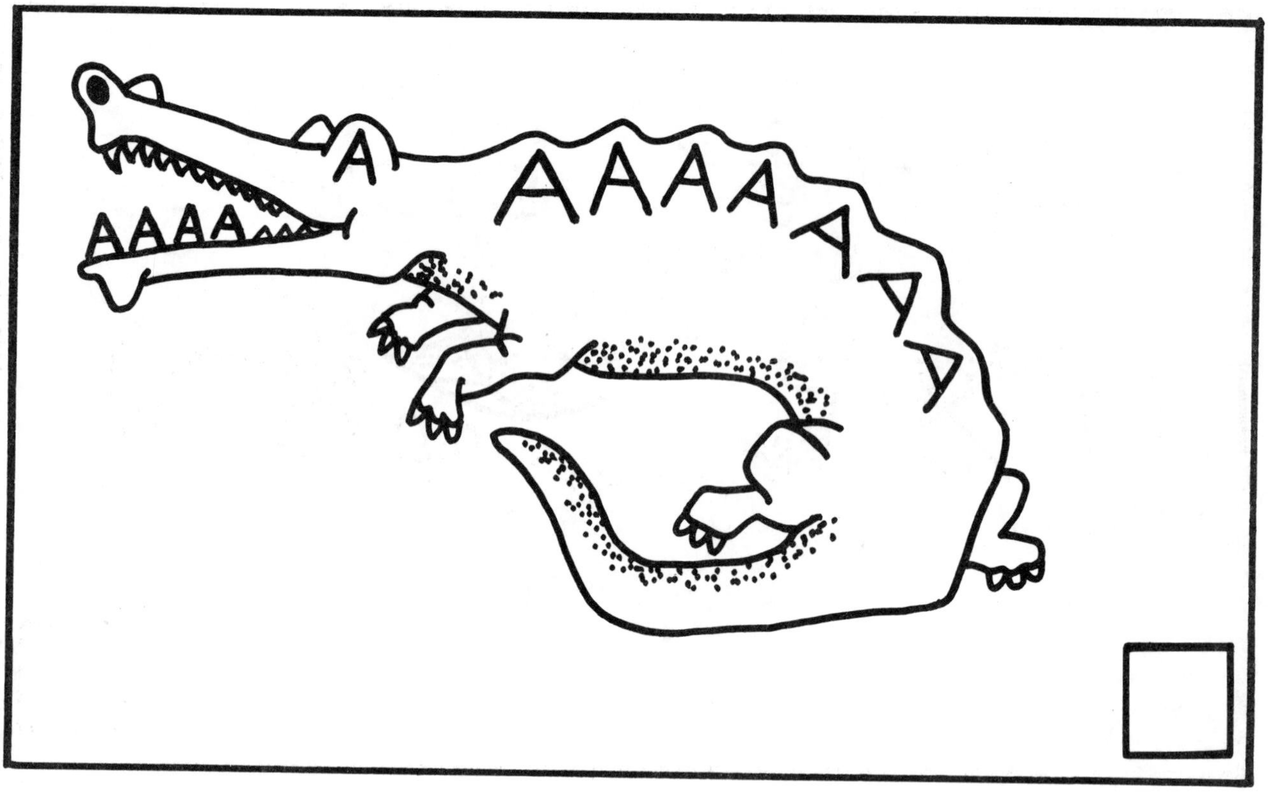

Color the beaver and write the number of B's in the box.

Name ____

Color the octopus and write the number of O's in the box.

Color the giraffe and write the number of G's in the box.

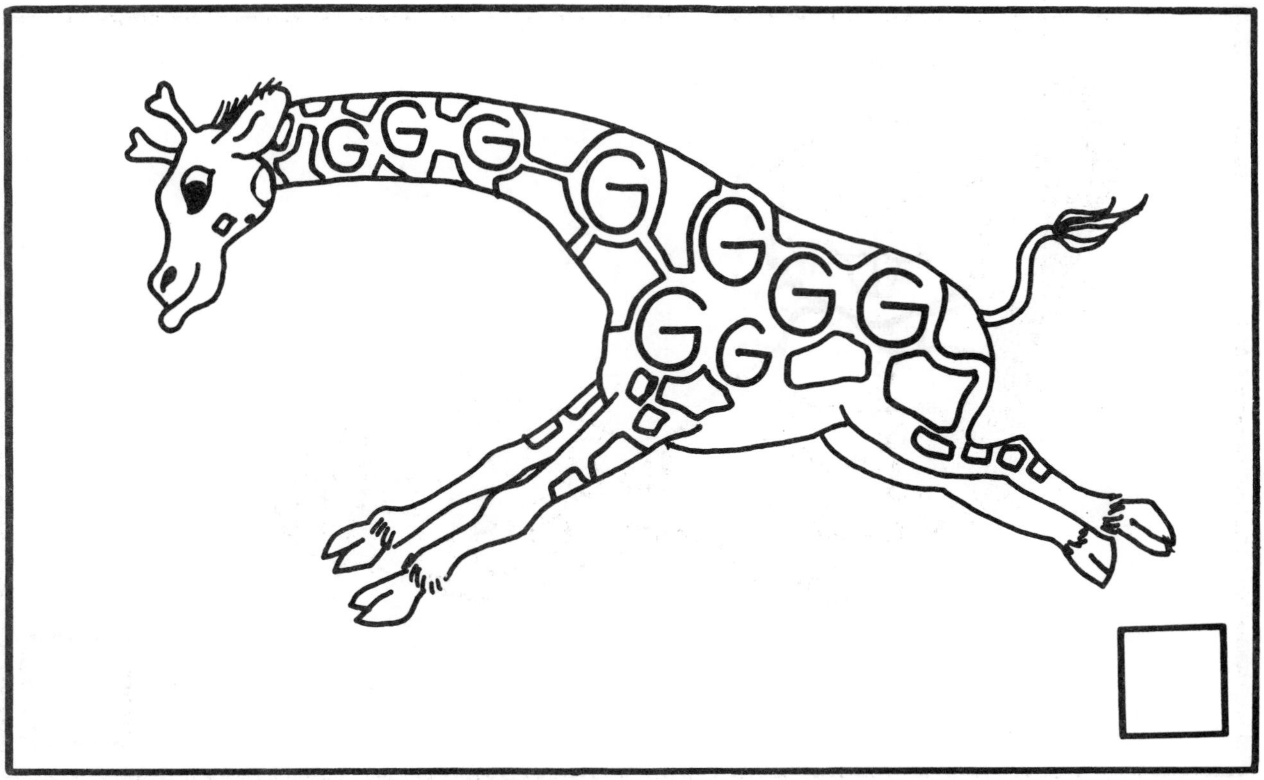

Name ______________________________

Color the tiger and write the number of T's in the box.

Color the peacock and write the number of P's in the box.

Name ____________________

In each row, circle the letters that are exactly the same as the first letter in the row.

N	N	H	N	M	N
R	B	R	R	P	R
G	Q	C	G	O	G
W	W	V	W	M	W
P	R	P	P	D	P
F	E	F	H	F	F

Name ______________________________

Circle the twins in each row.

1. 

2. 

3. 

4. 

Name ______________________________

Circle the twins in each row.

Find the letters. Color them red.

A 5 △ W F

☺ T Z □ H

B 4

8 D ⬡ C J

G ◇ 1 R 3 I

6 X L P N V

Y S

♡ U 7

E Q O ⬡

2 ☆ M K

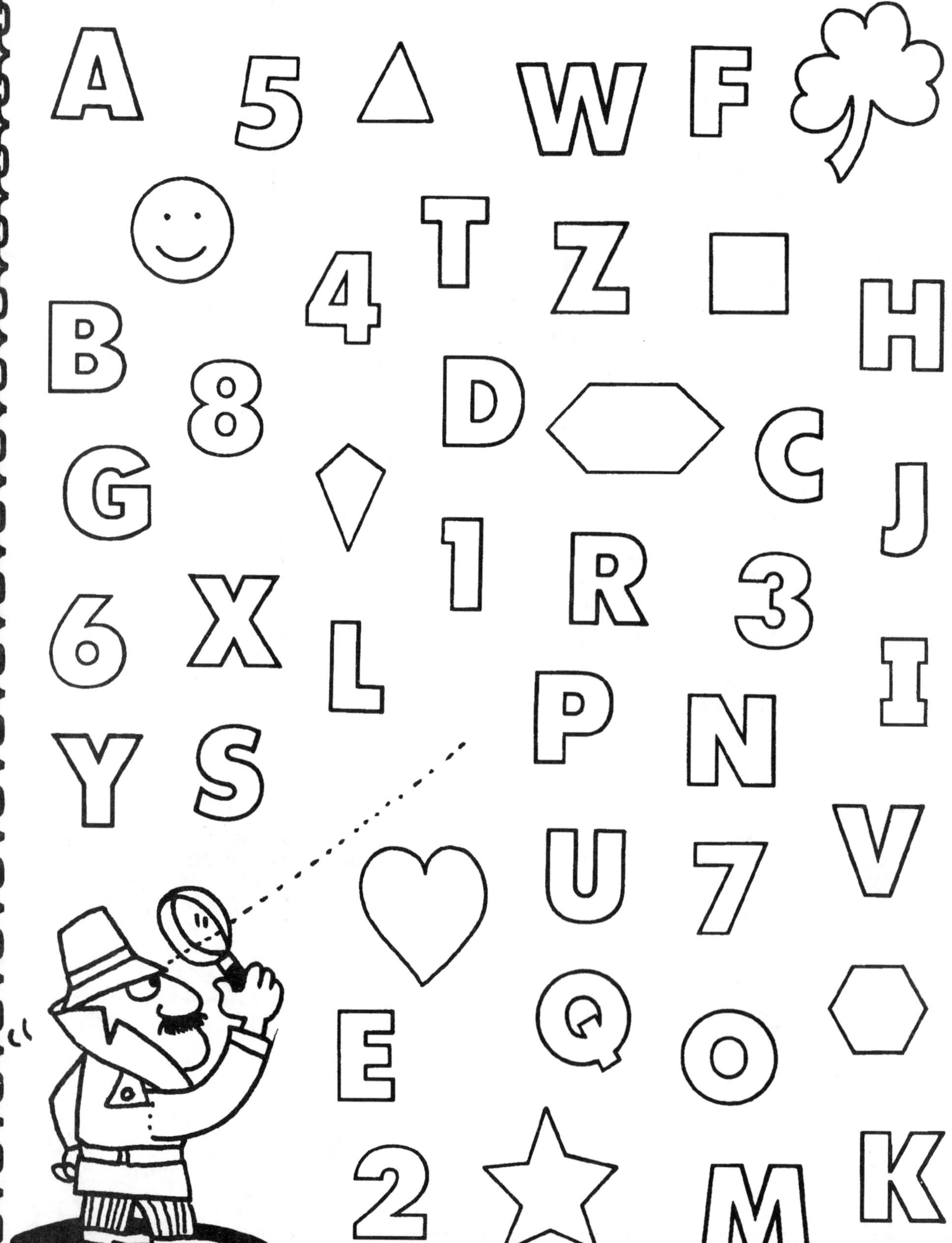

Name ________________________________

Color the picture and circle these hidden letters: **H, I, J, L, P, Q, U, W** and **Z.**

Name ______________________________

Look! All the capital letters are hidden in this picture.
Start with **A** and find them all!
Mark over them with your crayon.

Name ____

Color the picture and circle these hidden letters: **G, Z, L, A, H, F, N, Y, K, C, E, V, S, O, R, B, W, M, D, T, X, P, U, Q, I, J.**

Name ______________________________

Write the hidden letters and color the children.

Name ____

Write the hidden letters and color the children.

Name ______________________________

Write the hidden letters and color the children.

Name ______________________________

Help the mouse get to the cheese by going the A-B-C way.

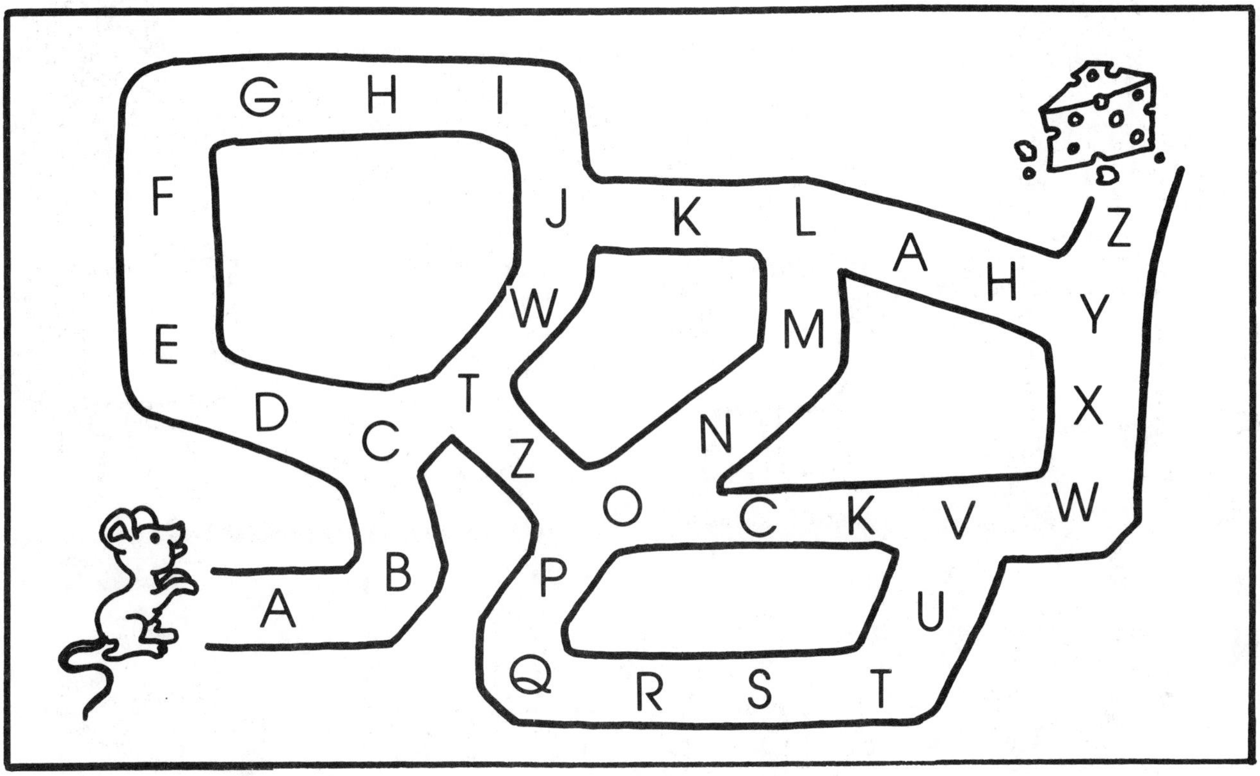

Help the monkey get to the banana by going the A-B-C way.

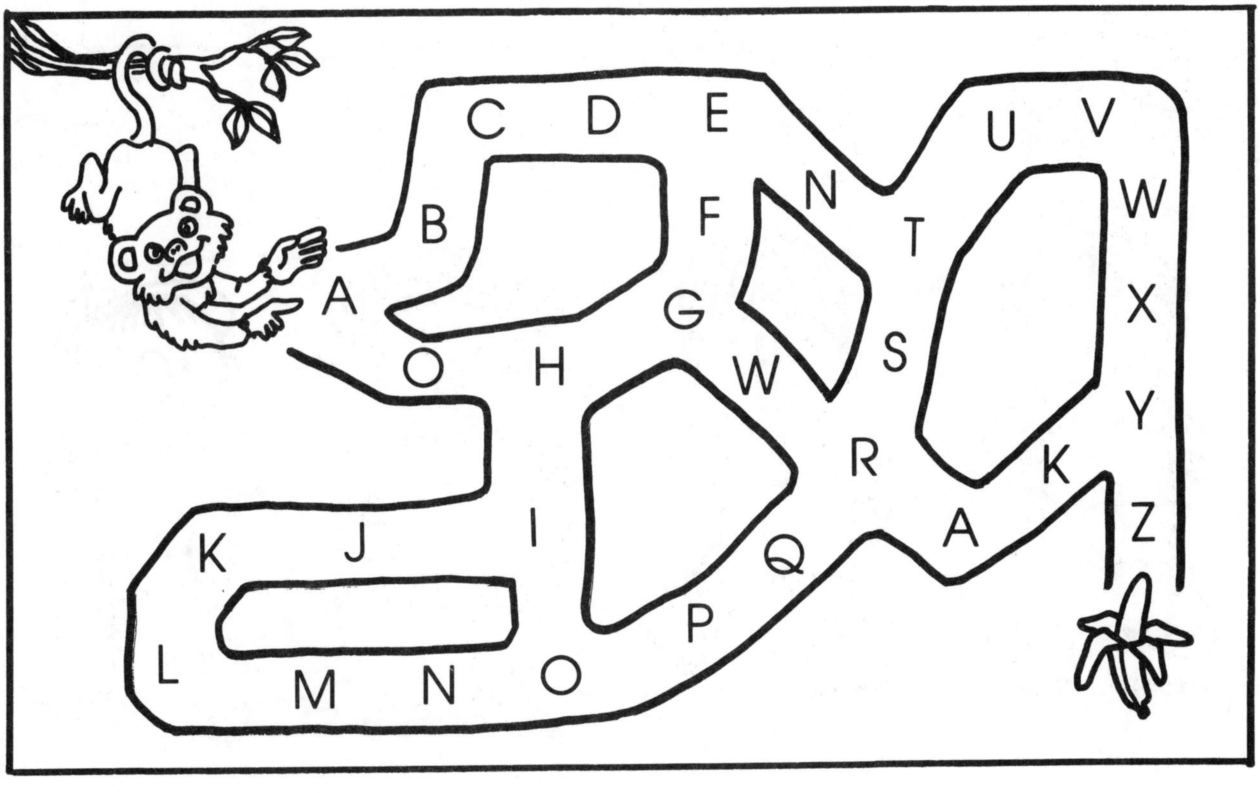

Name ____

Finish the alphabet.

Name ____________________

Can you write all of the capital letters?

A

D

Z

Name ____

Connect the dots the A-B-C way.

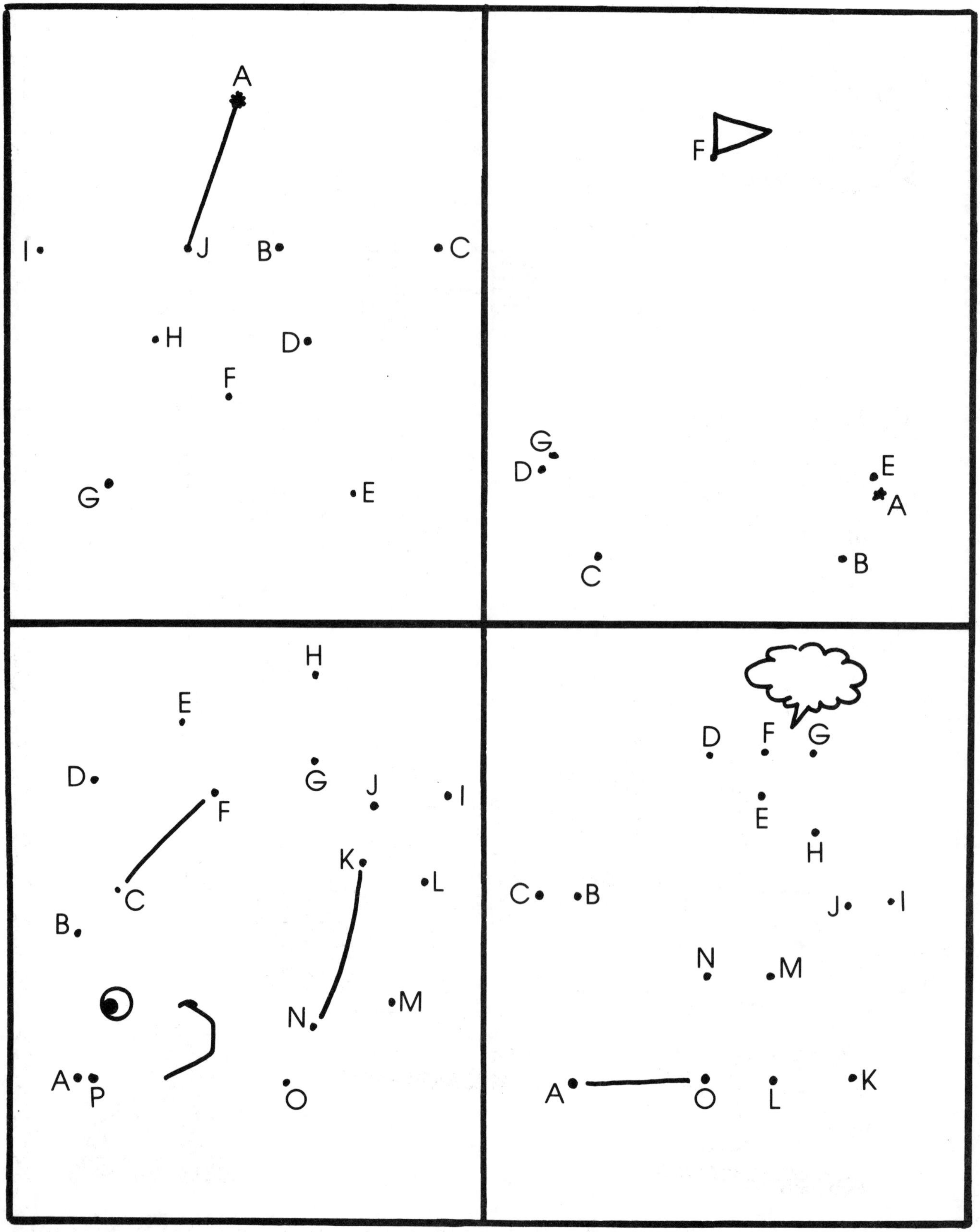

Name ______________________________________

Connect the dots starting with A.

Name ______________________________

Connect the dots starting with A.

Goldilocks

This one is just too soft.

Name ____________________

Connect the dots from A to Z.

Name ____________________

Connect the dots from A to Z.

Name ____________________

Skill: Upper-case alphabet—A to Z

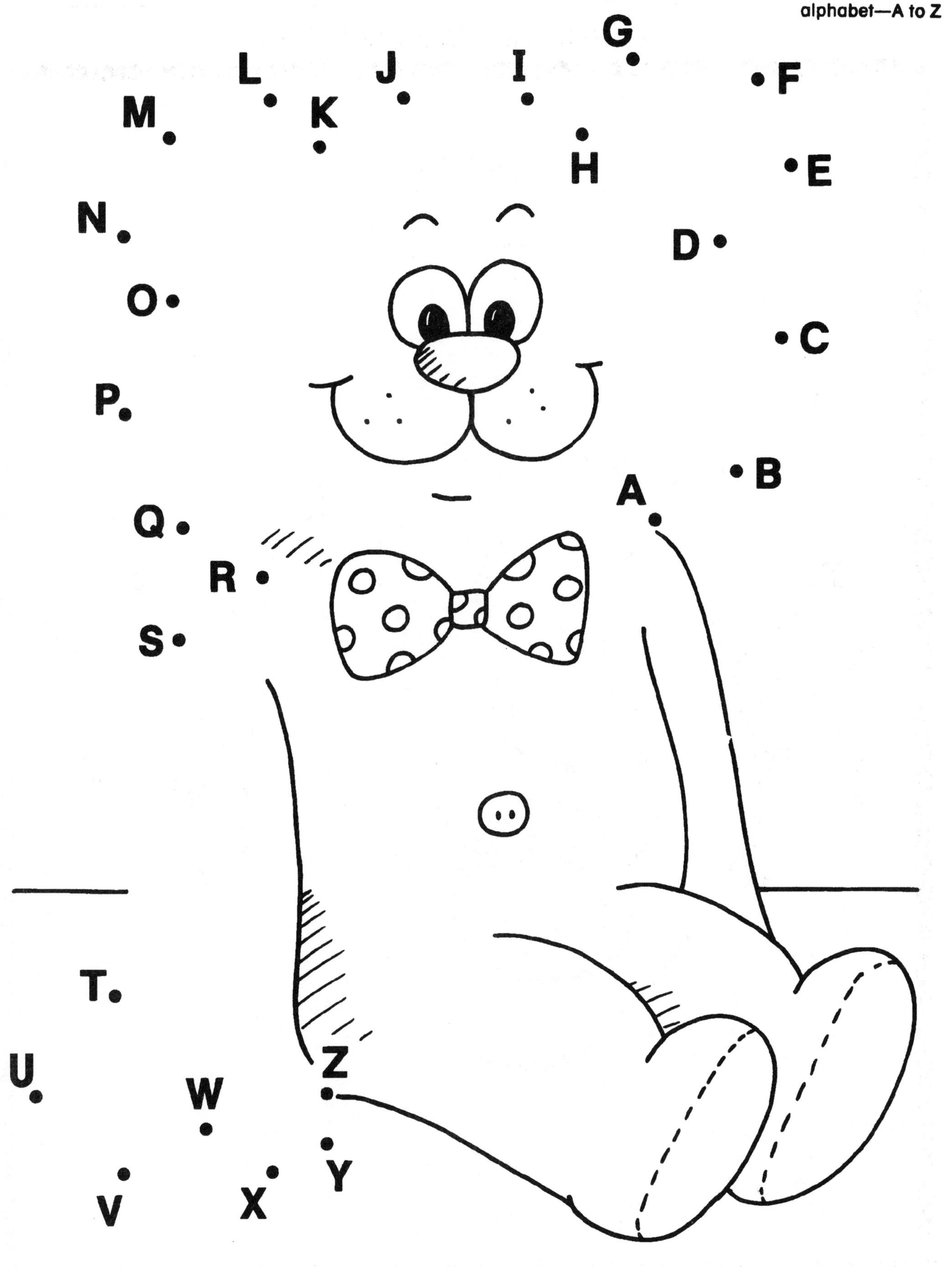

Name ______________________________

Skill: Upper-case alphabet—A to Z

Name ______________________________

Skill: Upper-case alphabet—A to Z

Name ____ Skill: Upper-case alphabet—A to Z

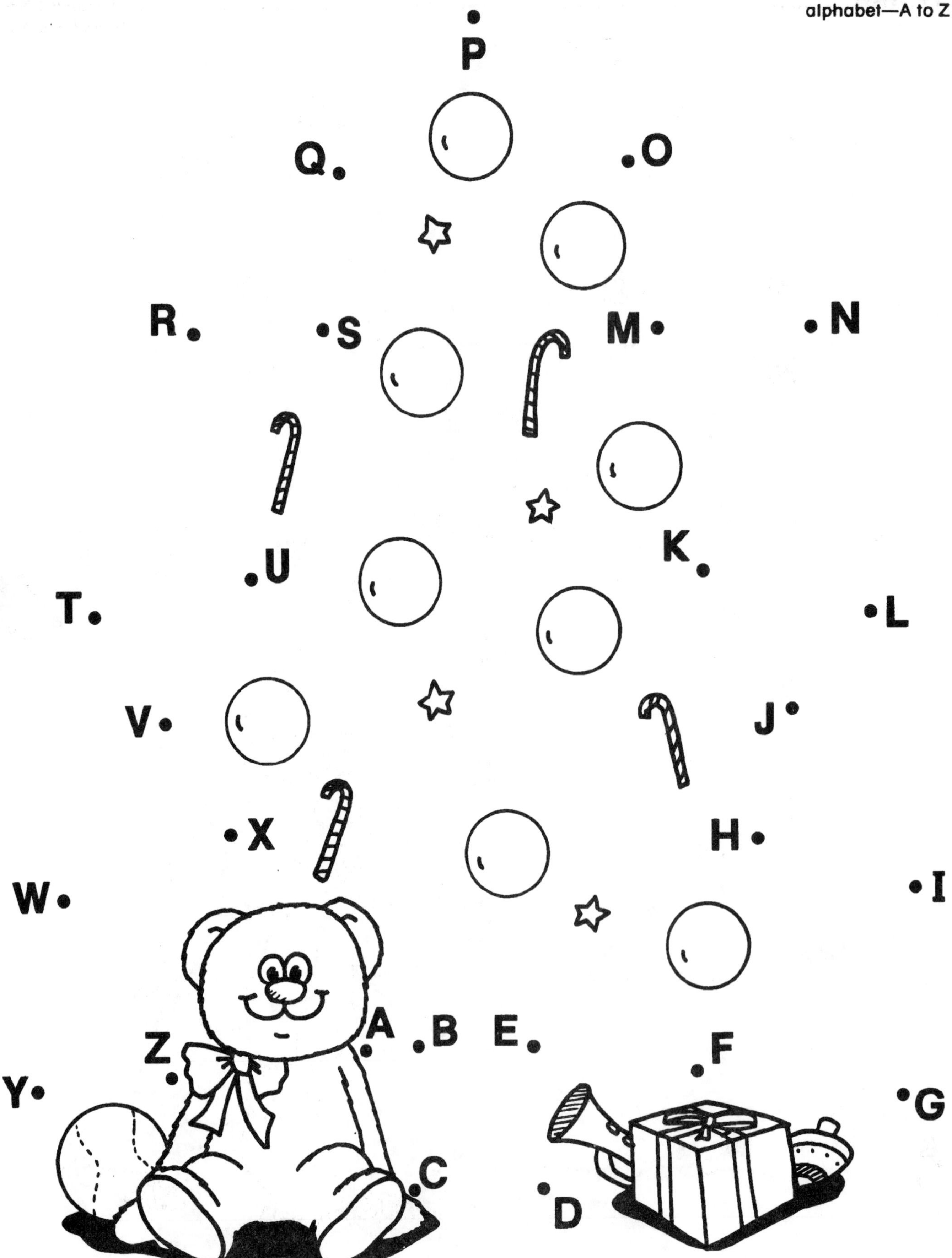

Name ____ Skill: Upper-case alphabet—A to Z

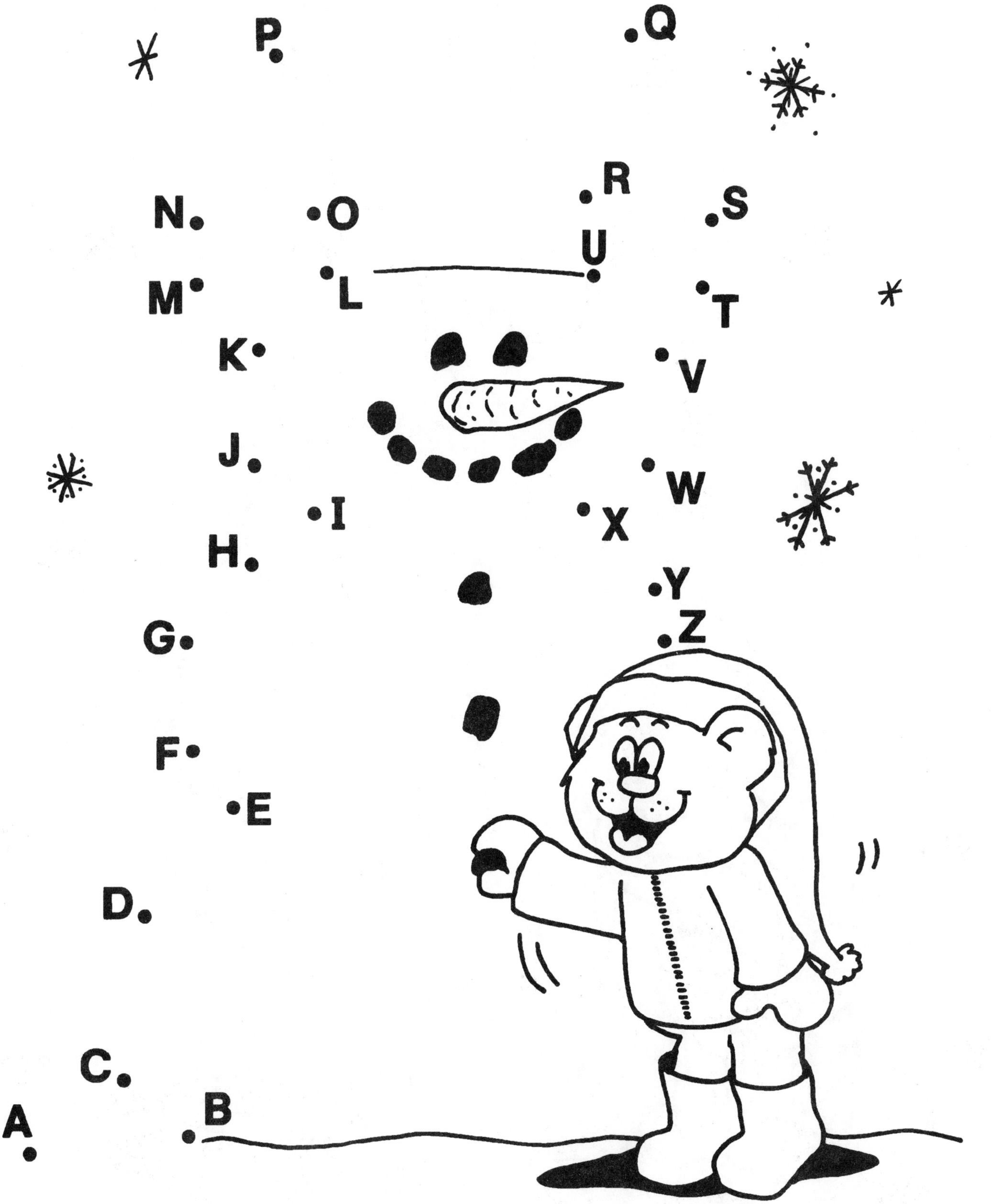

Name ____________________

Skill: Upper-case alphabet—A to Z

Name ______________________________ Skill: Upper-case alphabet—A to Z

Name ______________________________

Skill: Upper-case alphabet—A to Z

Name ____ Skill: Upper-case alphabet—A to Z

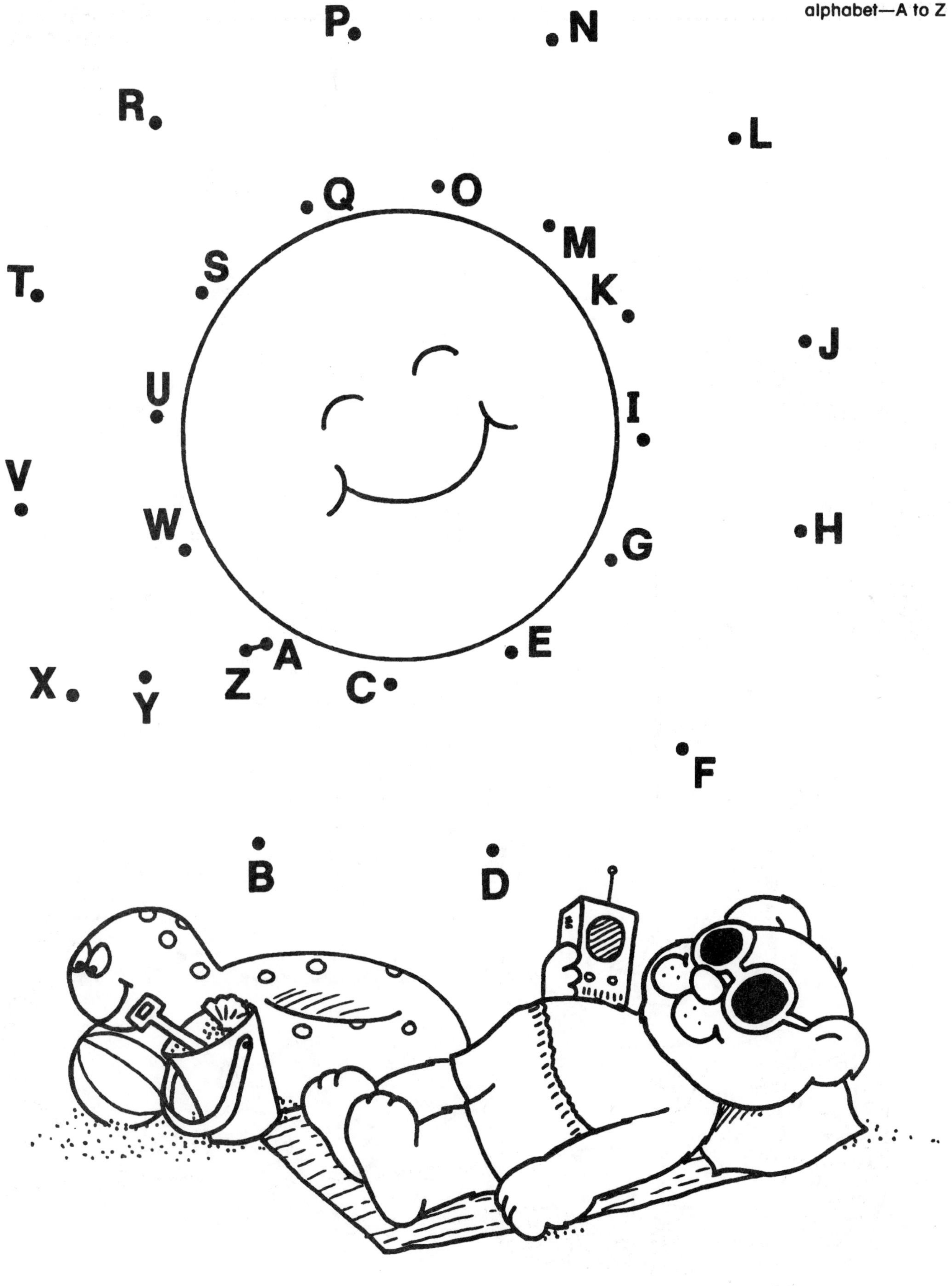

Name ______________________________

Skill: Upper-case alphabet—A to Z

Name ______________________________

Copy the sample letters.

a a   b b   c c   d d

e e   f f   g g   h h

i i   j j   k k   l l

m m   n n   o o   p p

q q   r r   s s   t t

u u   v v   w w

x x   y y   z z

Name ____________________

Say the name of each letter as you trace it.

a b c d

e f g h i j

k l m n o p

q r s t u v

w x y z

Name ____________________

Trace the lower case letter that has the same name as the capital letter.

A a	B b	C c
D d	E e	F f
G g	H h	I i
J j	K k	L l

Name ______________________________

Trace the lower case letters.

	M m	N n
O o	P p	Q q
R r	S s	T t
U u	V v	W w
X x	Y y	Z z

Name ____________________

Draw a line to the right bottle.

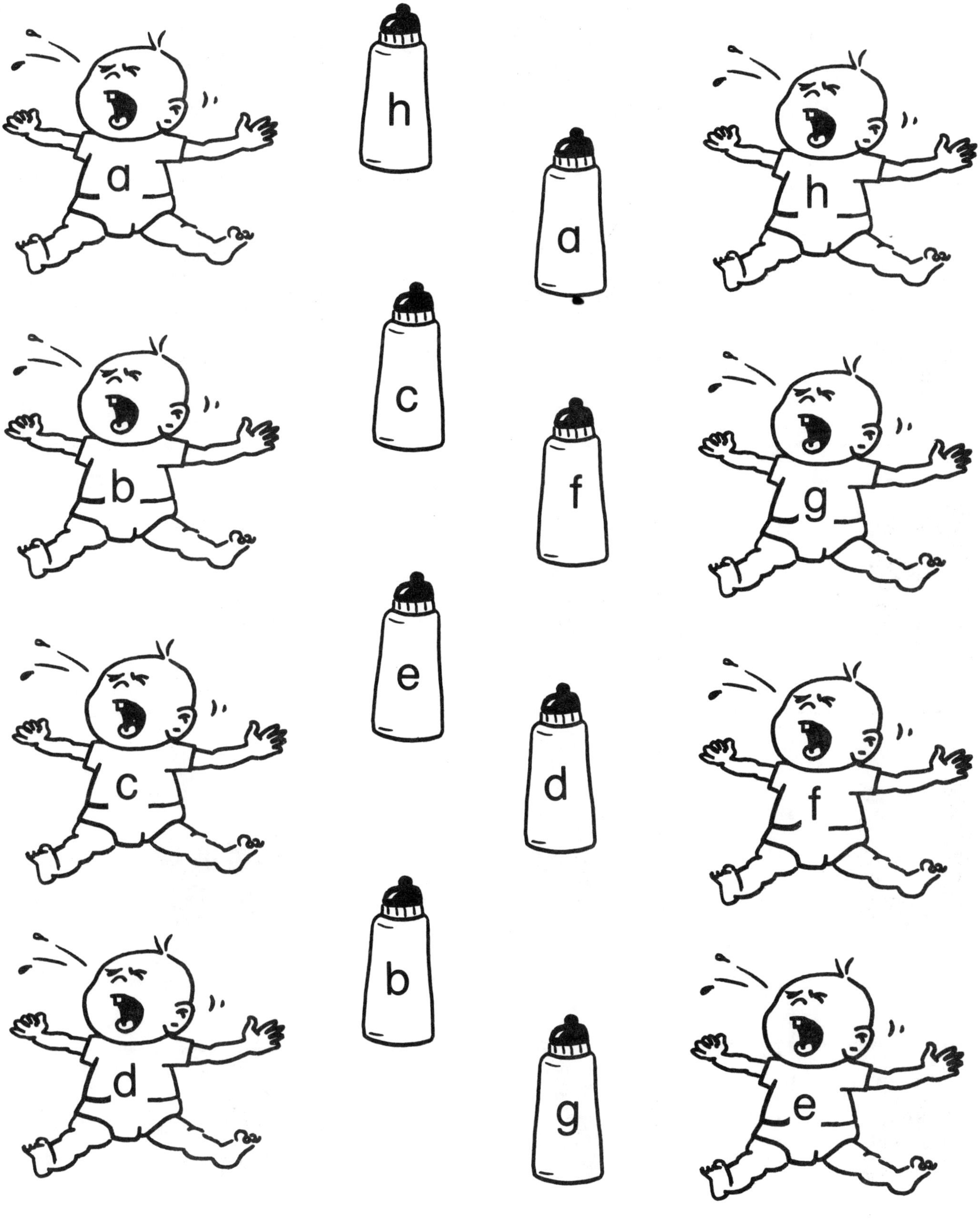

Name ______________________________

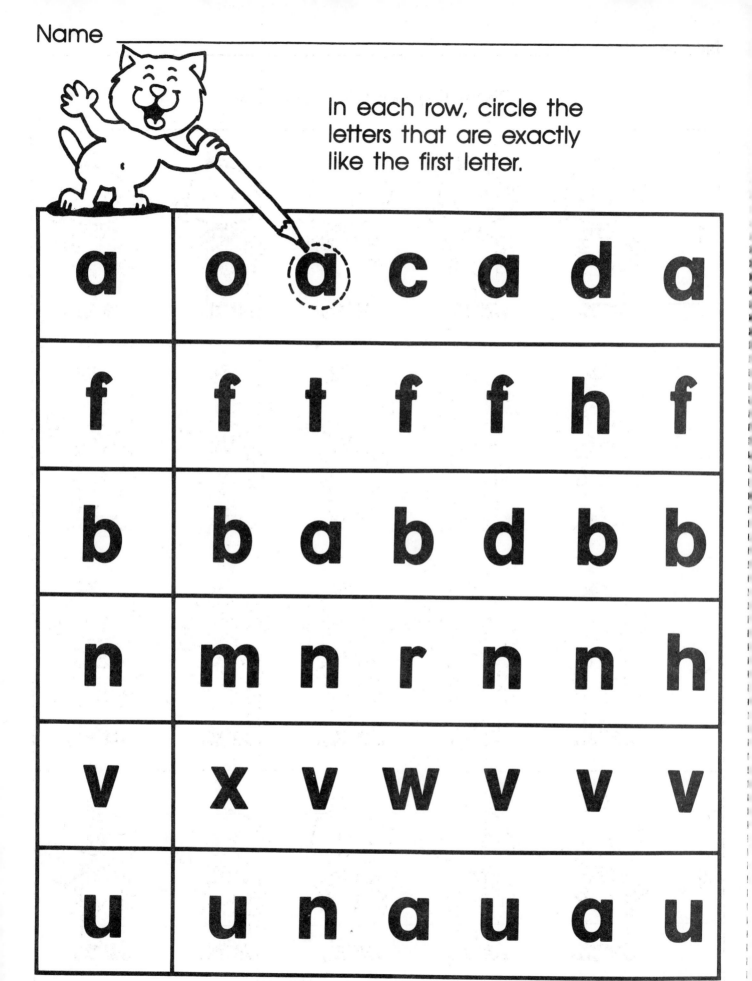

In each row, circle the letters that are exactly like the first letter.

a	o	a	c	a	d	a
f	f	t	f	f	h	f
b	b	a	b	d	b	b
n	m	n	r	n	n	h
v	x	v	w	v	v	v
u	u	n	a	u	a	u

Name ________________________________

Circle the twins in each row.

1.

2.

3.

4.

Name ______________________________

Circle the twins in each row.

7

Name ______________________________

Find the letters.
Color them green.

Name ______________________________

Write the hidden letters and color the animals.

Name ______________________________

Write the hidden letters and color the animals.

Name ____________________

Write the hidden letters and color the animals.

Name ______________________________

Help the pig get to his food by going the A-B-C way.

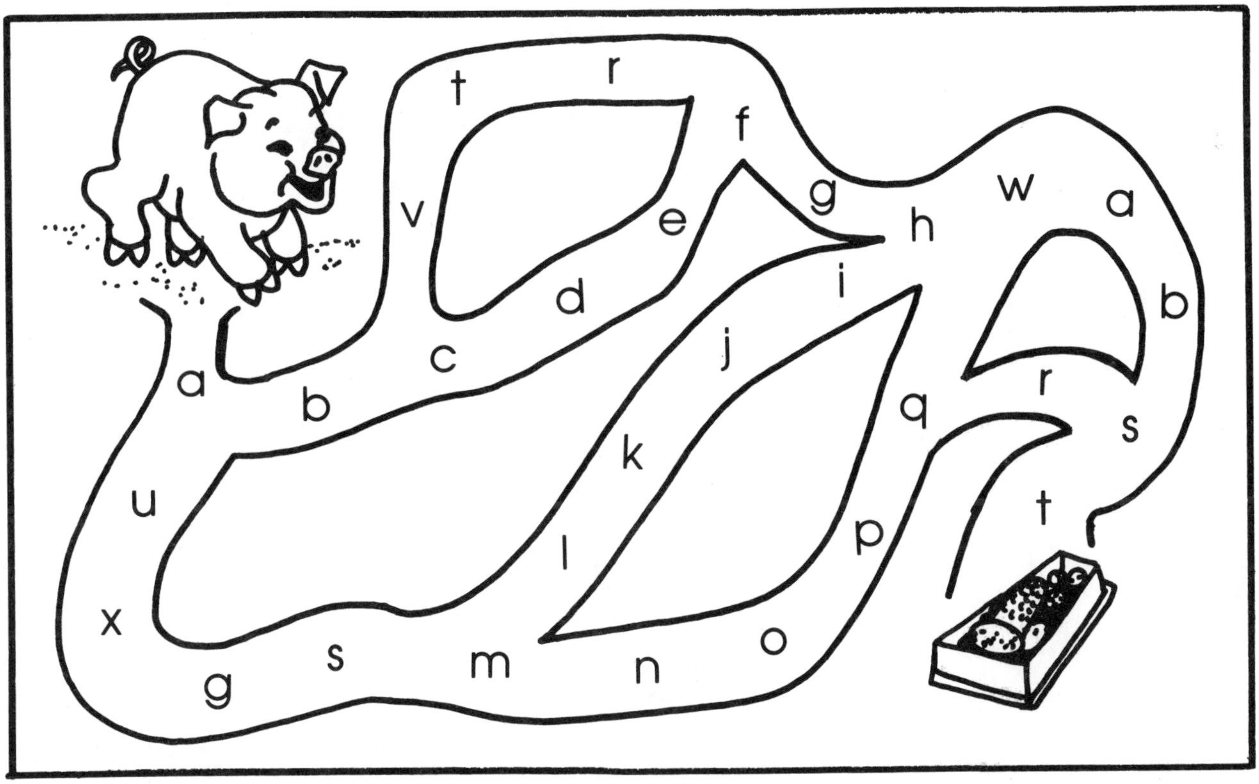

Help the camel get to the water by going the A-B-C way.

Name ______________________________

Help the cat get to the fish by going the a-b-c way.

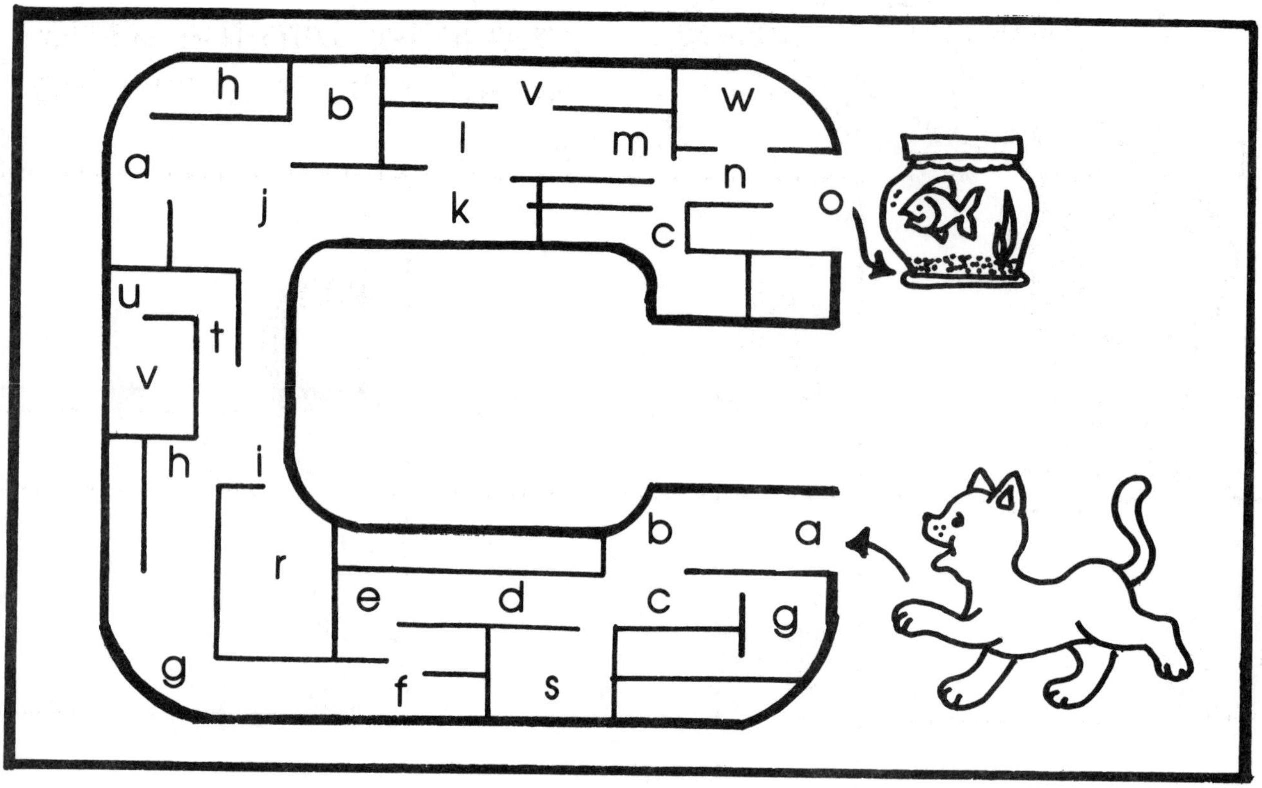

Help the dog get to the doghouse by going the a-b-c way.

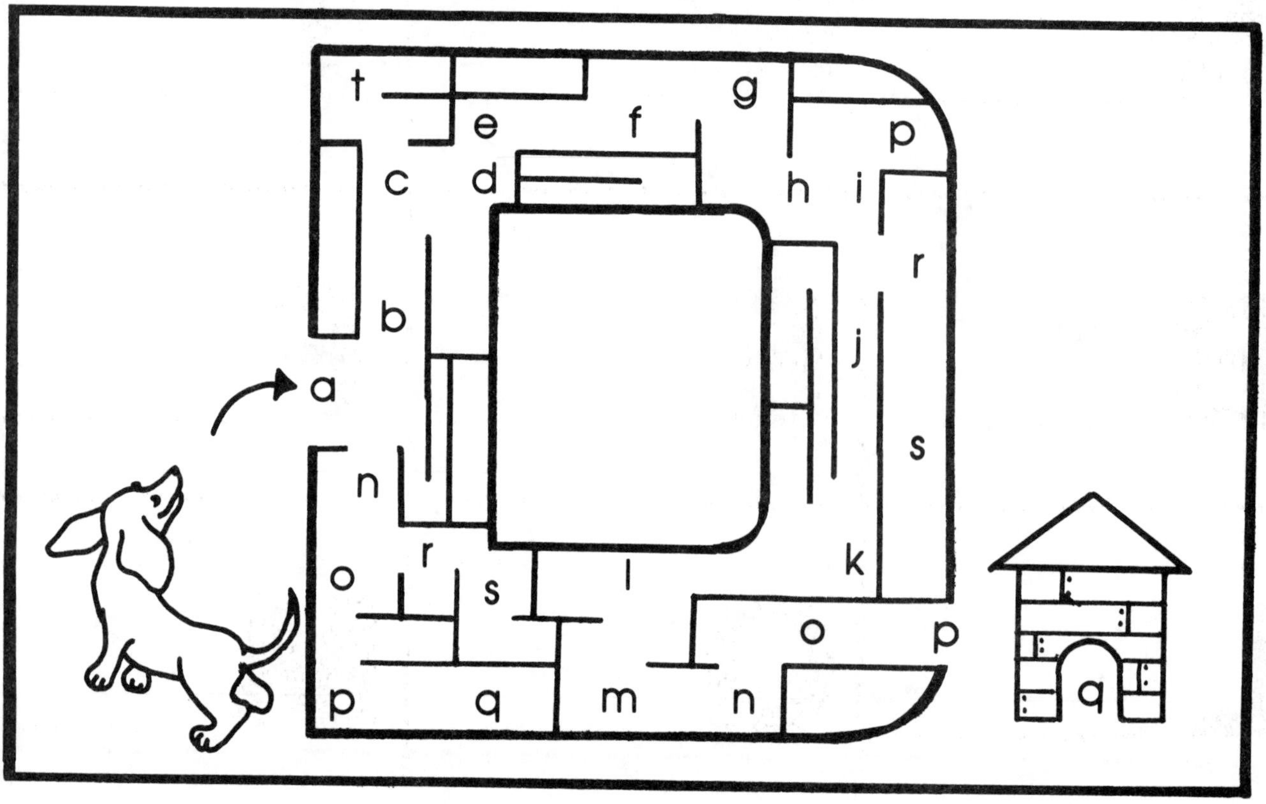

Name ____

Can you remember the lower case letter with the **same name**? Write it on the line.

	A ____	D ____
G ____	H ____	I ____
N ____	R ____	T ____
B ____	E ____	F ____
L ____	Q ____	M ____

Name ______________________________

Finish the alphabet.

Name ____

Can you write all the lower case letters?

		a		
d			g	
		z		

Name ______________________________

Circle the letters in our names and color us.

Name ______________________________

Circle the letters in our names and color us.

Name ____________________

Circle the letters in our names and color us.

Name ________________________________

Connect the dots from a to z.

Name ____

Connect the dots from a to z.

Name ______________________________

Connect the dots from a to z.

Name ____________________

Skill: Lower-case alphabet—a to z

Name ______________________________

Skill: Lower-case alphabet—a to z

Name ____

Skill: Lower-case alphabet—a to z

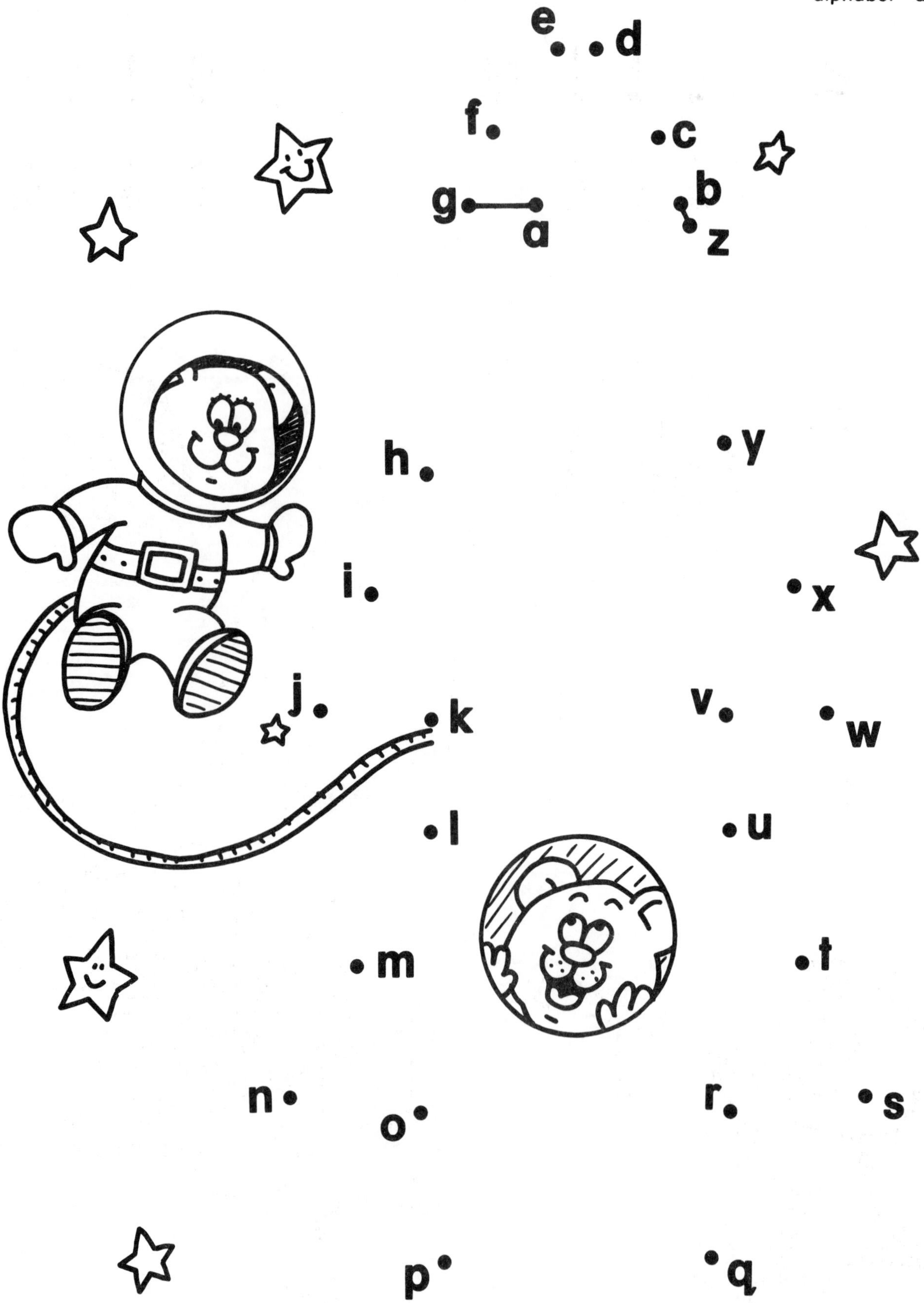

Name ______________________________

Skill: Lower-case alphabet—a to z

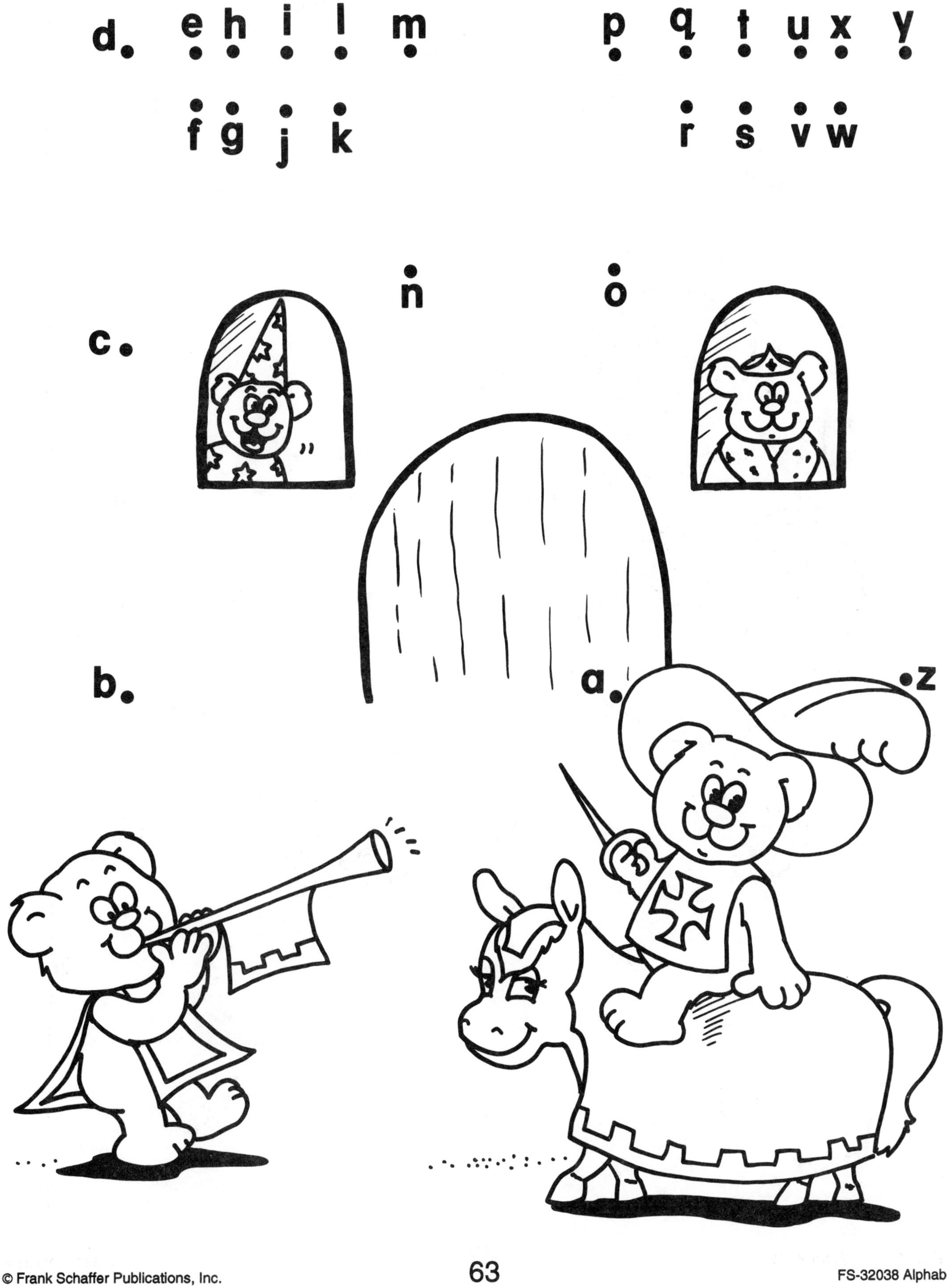

Name ______________________________

Skill: Lower-case alphabet—a to z

Name ______________________________ Skill: Lower-case alphabet—a to z

Name ____________________

Skill: Lower-case alphabet—a to z

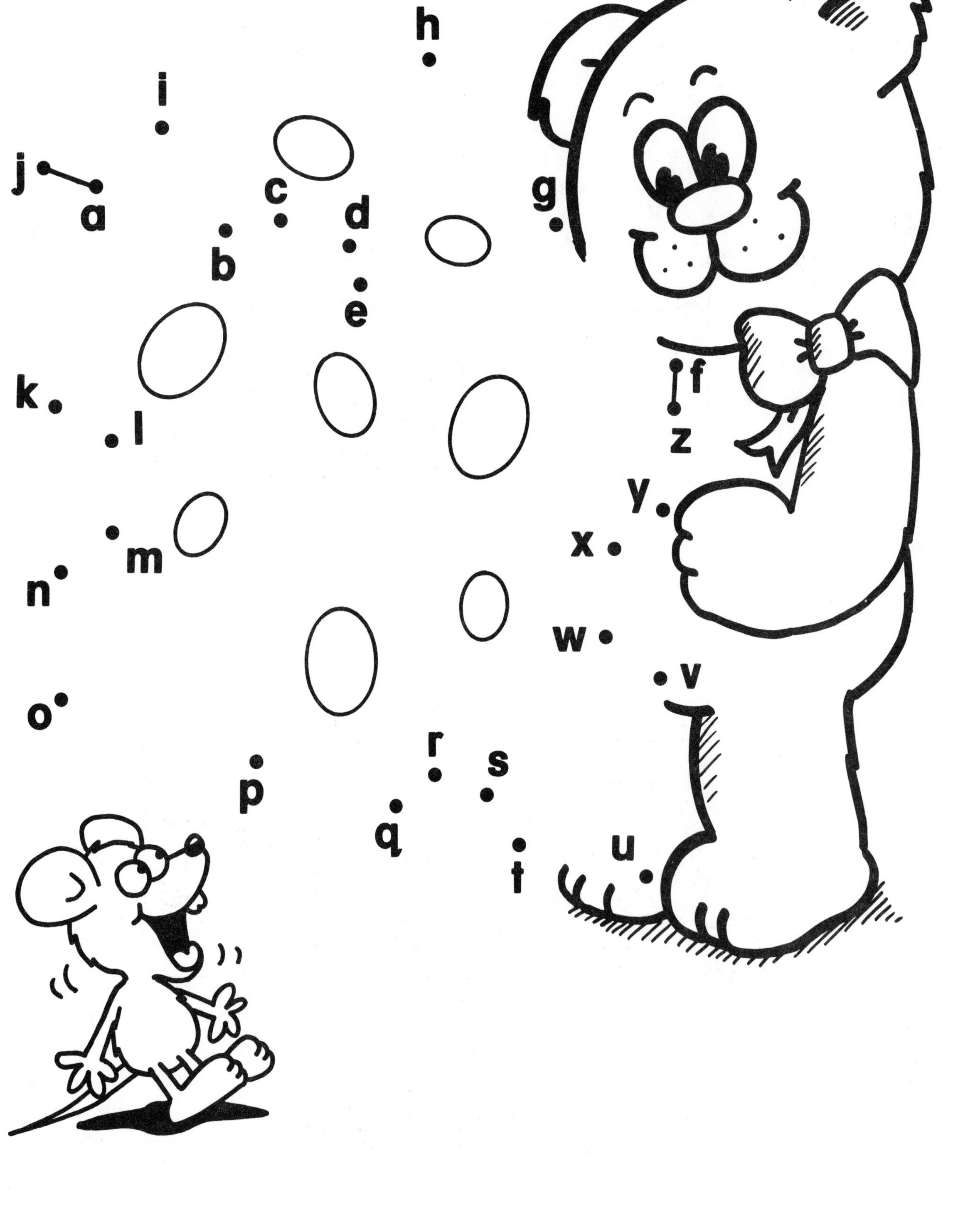

Name ______________________________

Skill: Lower-case alphabet—a to z

Name ______________________________

Skill: Lower-case alphabet—a to z

Name ______________________________

Skill: Lower-case alphabet—a to z

Name ______________________________

Connect the dots starting with A.

Name ____________________

Connect the dots starting with A.

Name ______________________________

Practice the alphabet.

A B C D E F G

H I J K L M

N O P Q R S

T U V W X Y Z

a b c d e f g

h i j k l m

n o p q r s

t u v w x y z

Name ______________________________

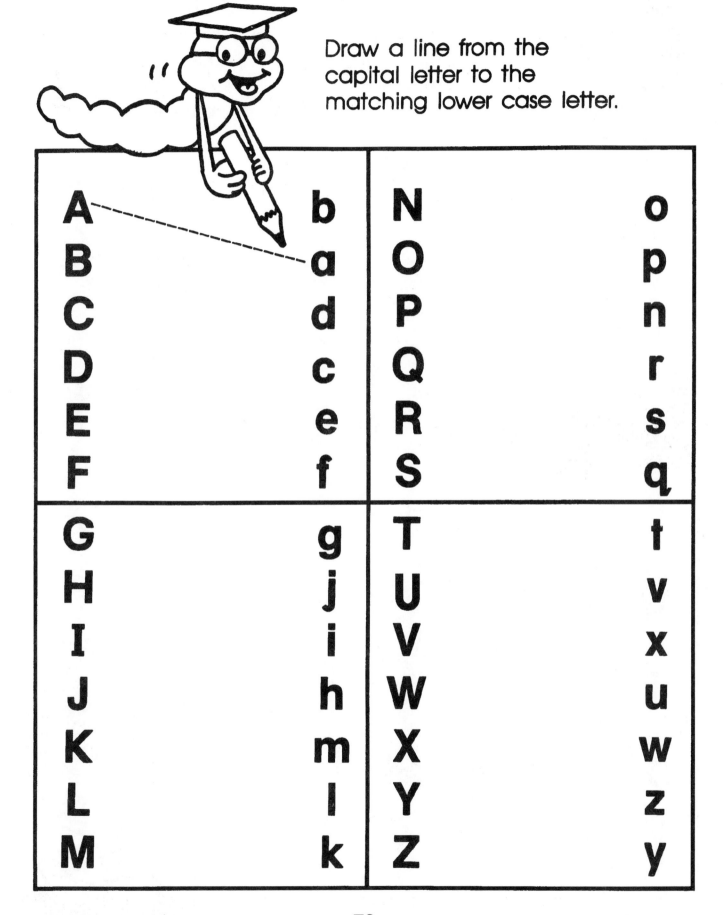

Draw a line from the capital letter to the matching lower case letter.

A	b	N	o
B	a	O	p
C	d	P	n
D	c	Q	r
E	e	R	s
F	f	S	q
G	g	T	t
H	j	U	v
I	i	V	x
J	h	W	u
K	m	X	w
L	l	Y	z
M	k	Z	y

Name ______________________________

Draw a line to the right pet.

Name ____________________

Draw a line to the right little brother.

Name ______________________________

Mystery Picture

Color the spaces with upper case letters **green**. Color the spaces with lower case letters **brown**.

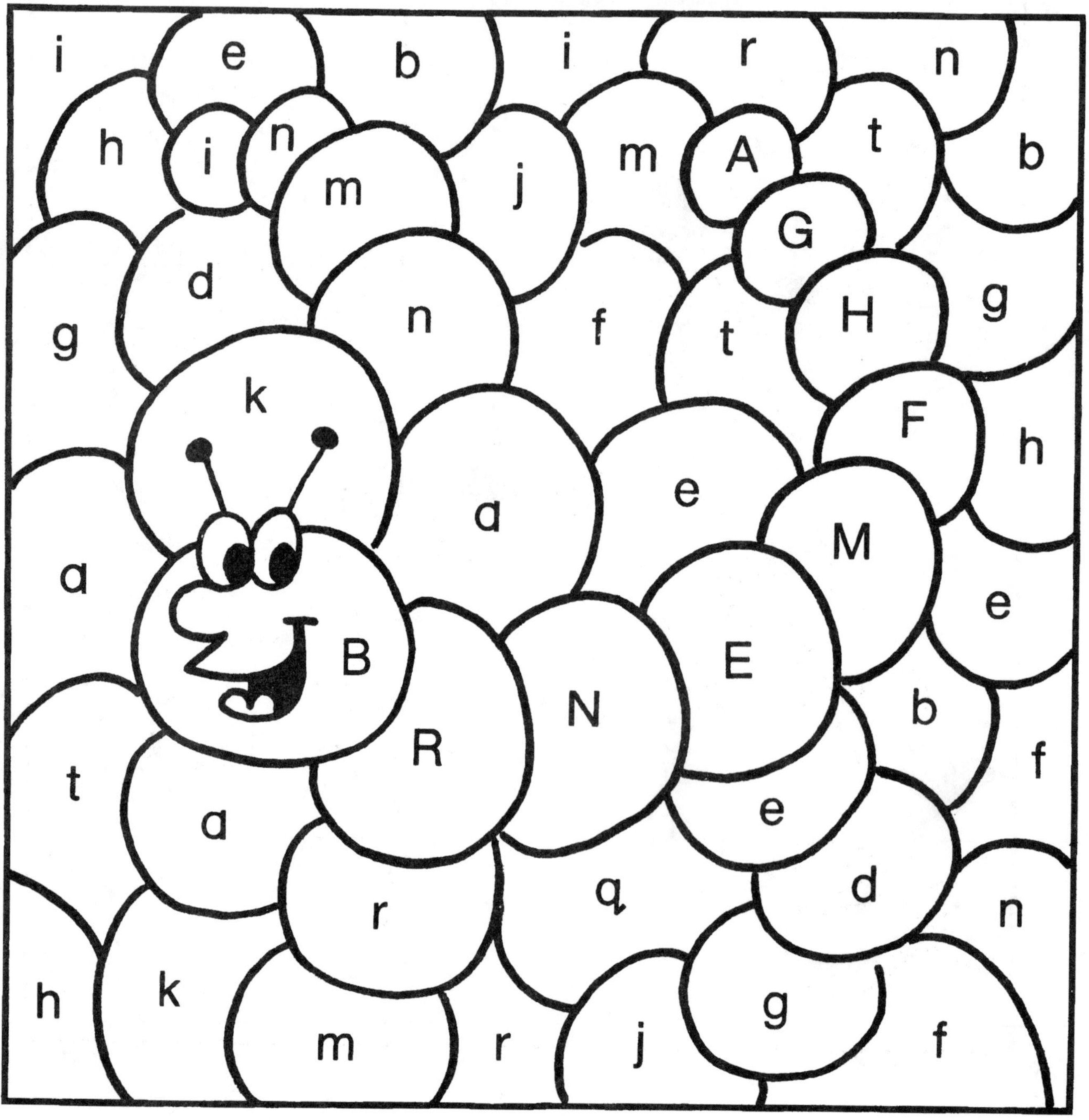

Name ______________________________

Color the picture and circle these hidden letters: **Y, A, W, t, H, S, j, L, d, N** and **X.**

Name ______________________________

Write the missing letter in each box.

		A	B			E
F			I			L
M				Q		S
T			W			Z

		a	b			e
f			i		k	
m				q		s
t		v				z

Name ____

Circle the letters in our names and color us.

A ☆ F ☆ G ☆ H ☆ I ☆ J ☆ V ☆ W ☆ X ☆ E ☆ B ☆ D ☆ I

B ☆ C ☆ D ☆ L ☆ M ☆ K ☆ J ☆

N ☆ Q ☆ O ☆ P ☆ R ☆ S ☆ T

CONGRATULATIONS!

____

Name

can correctly name all of the upper case letters in the alphabet.

____

Official signature

☆ L ☆ Y ☆ N ☆ E ☆ F ☆ G ☆ Z ☆ X ☆ W ☆ V ☆ U ☆ T

a ☆ b ☆ e ☆ c ☆ f ☆ h ☆ d ☆ i ☆ k ☆ g ☆ j ☆ m

c ☆ d ☆ k ☆ l ☆ n ☆ o ☆ p

q ☆ r ☆ s ☆ t ☆ u ☆ v ☆ w

Congratulations!

____

Name

can correctly name all of the lower case letters in the alphabet.

____

Official signature

p ☆ q ☆ r ☆ s ☆ z ☆ u ☆ v ☆ w ☆ x ☆ y ☆ l ☆ w

Name ________________________

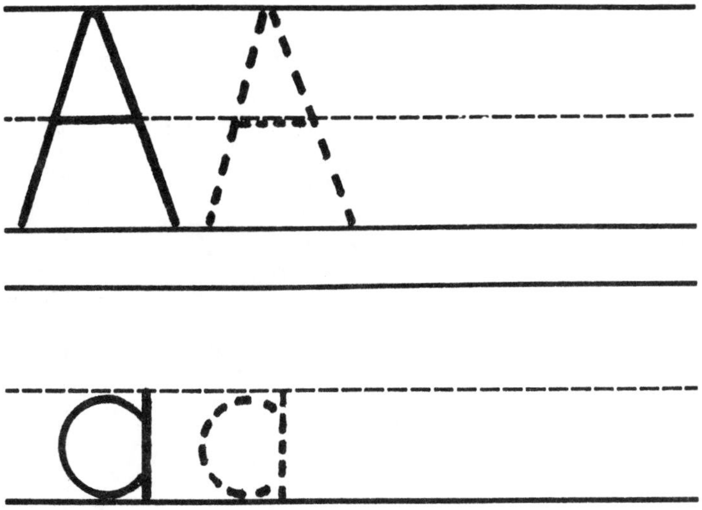

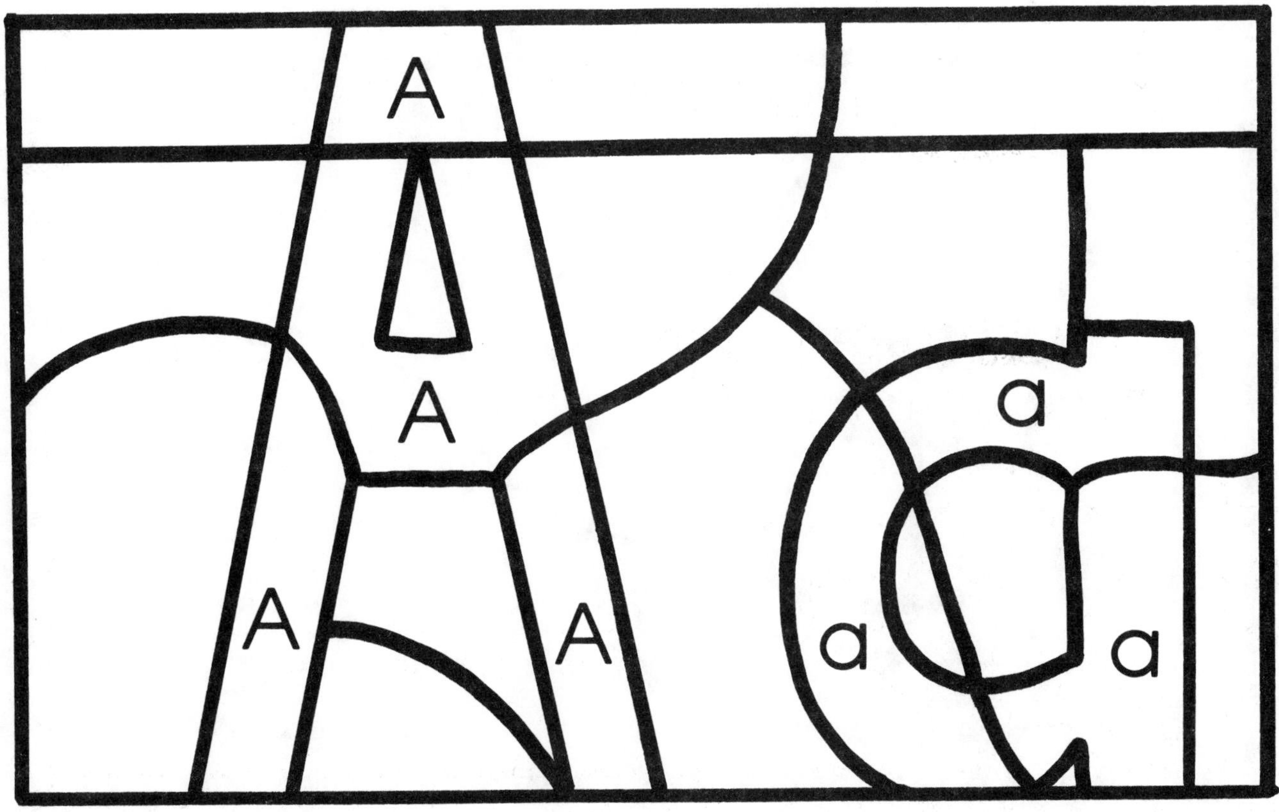

Name ______________________________

B B

b b

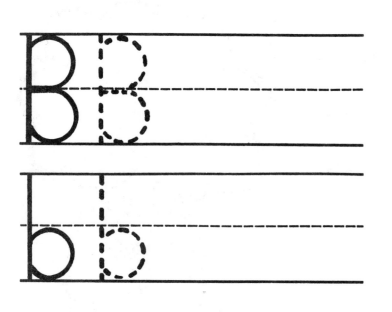

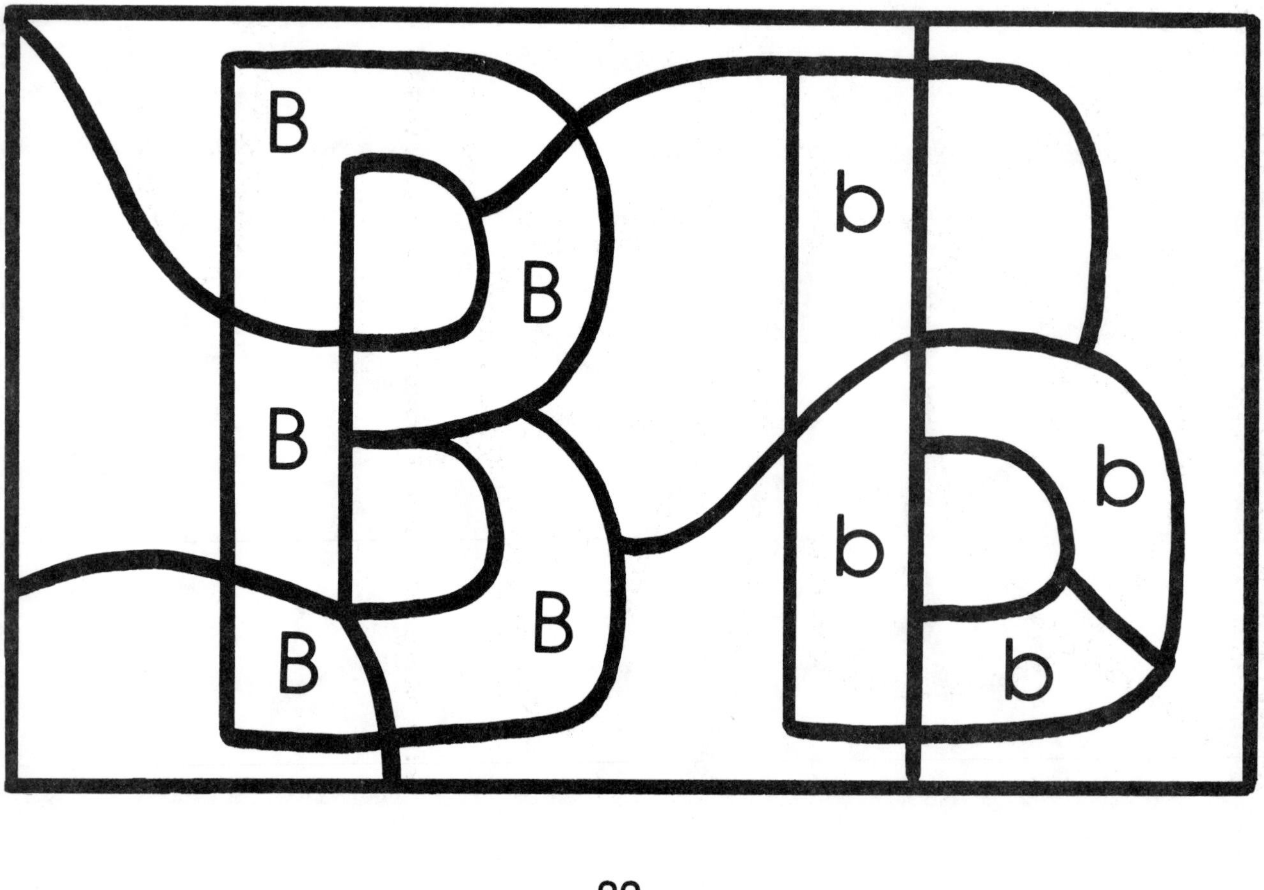

Name ____________________

C C

c c

Name

B

b

bee

C

c

cat

Name ______________________

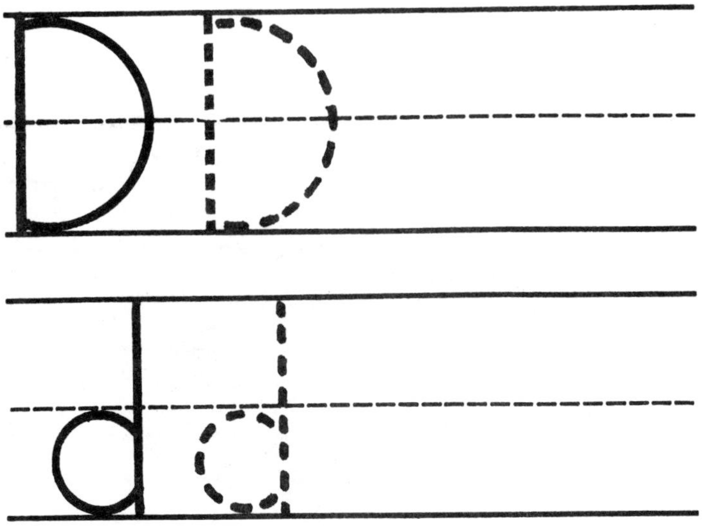

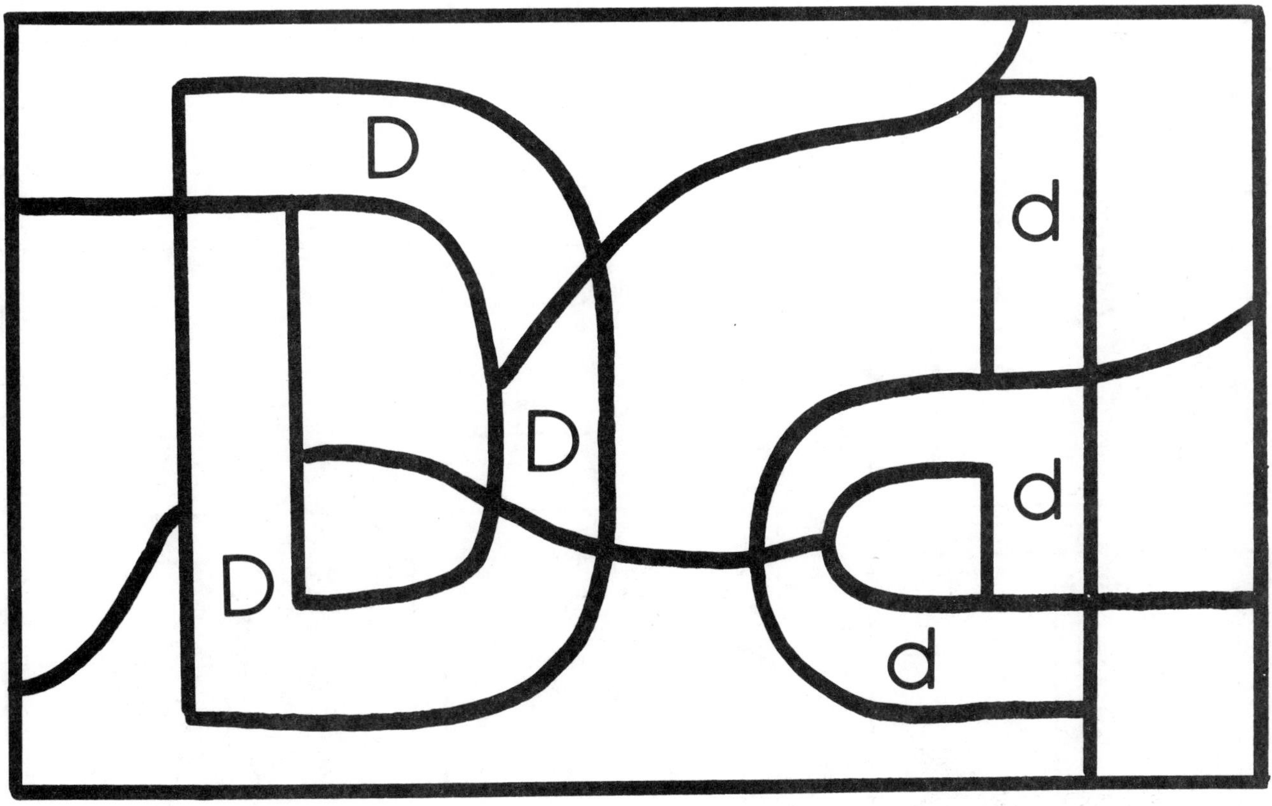

Name ______________________________ Initial Consonant d

D D

D

d d

d

Print the letter " **d** ".

Name ______________________________

Print the letter " **d** ".

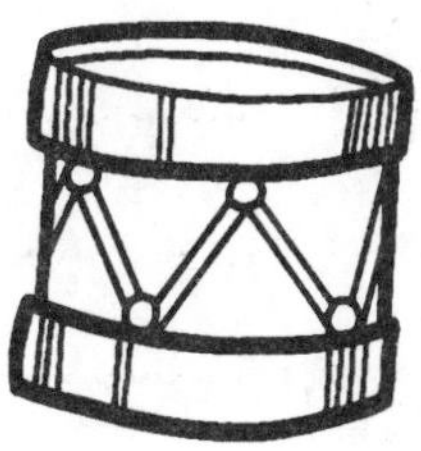

Name ________________________________

D

d

dog

E

e

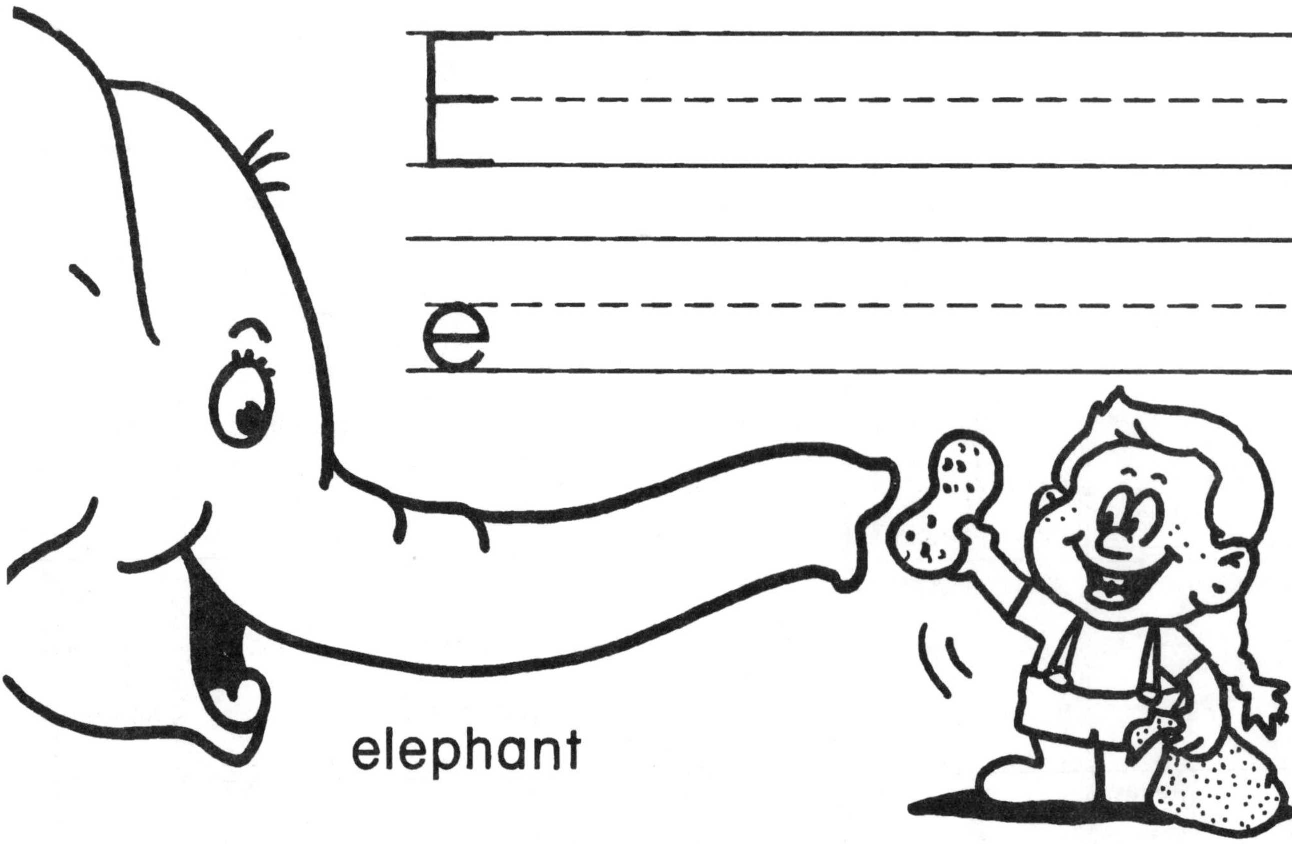

elephant

Name ____________________

E E

e e

F F

f f

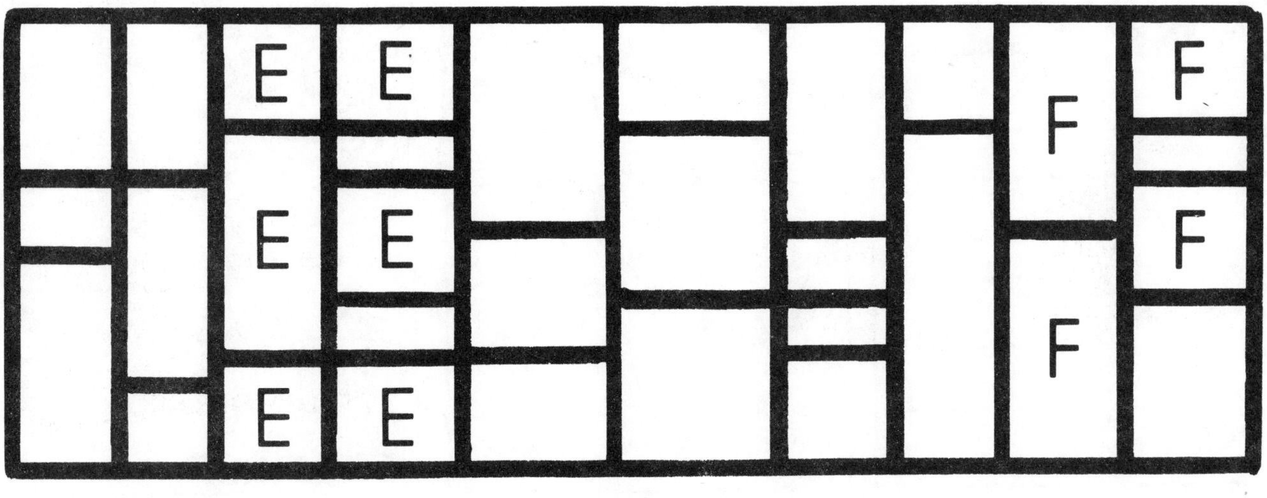

Name ______________________

Print the letter " **f** ".

5

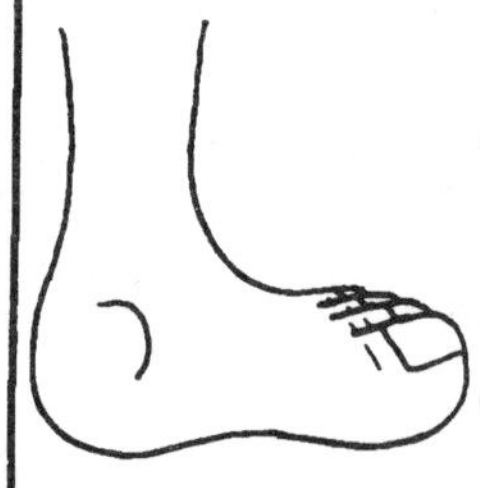

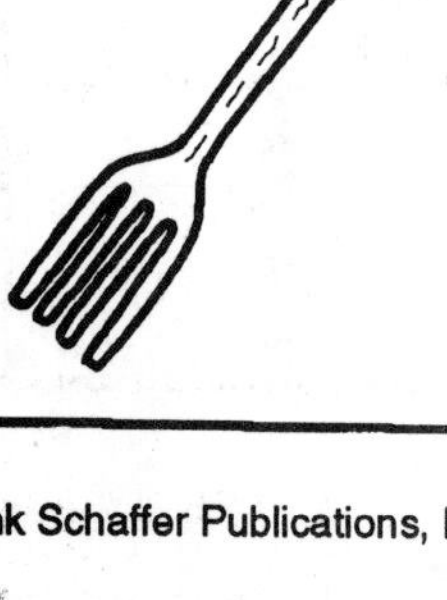

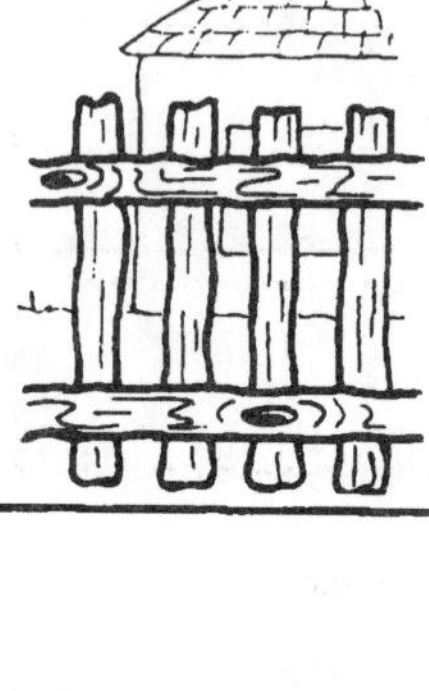

Name ______________________________

Print the letter " **f** ".

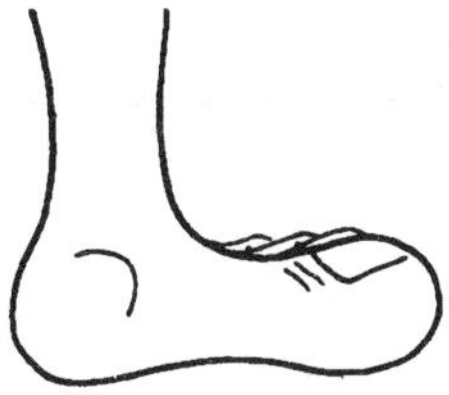

5

Name ______________________

Name ____

F

f

G

g

Name ______________________________

Draw a line to the letter with the same name.

A	b
B	d
C	a
D	c
E	f
F	e
G	g

Trace and name each letter.

C D A B F E G

c d a b f e g

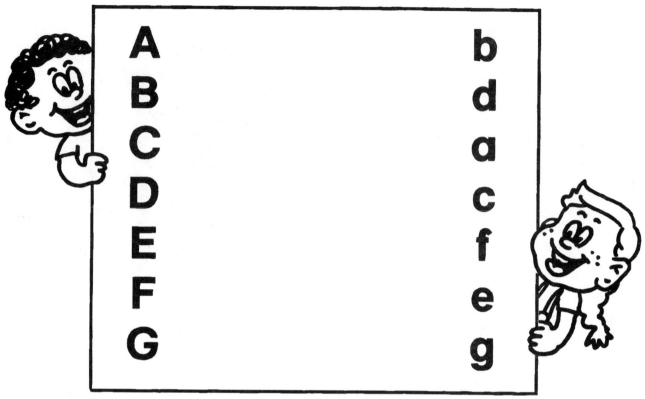

Name ______________________________

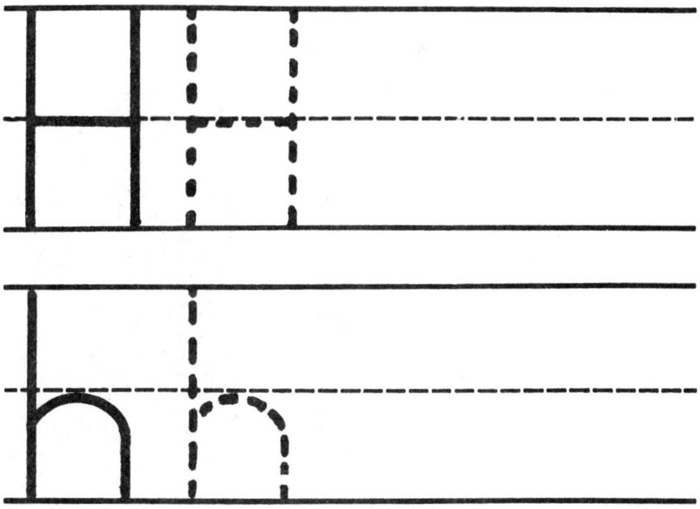

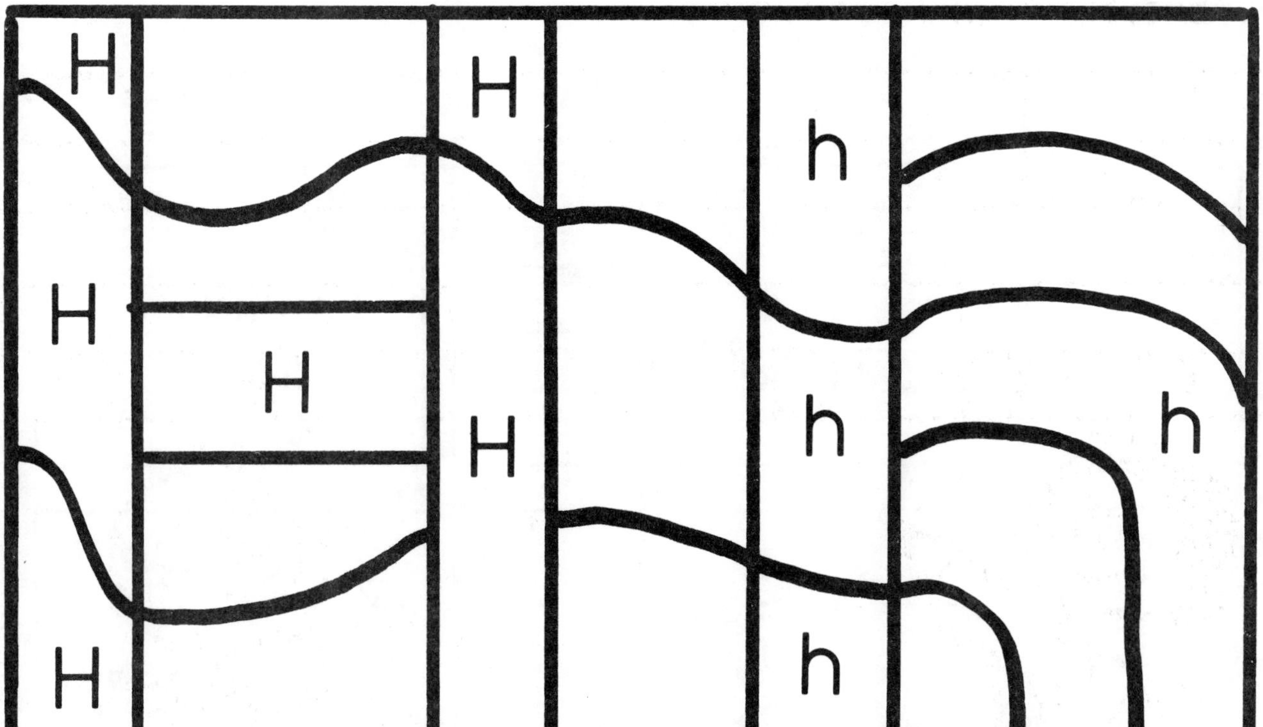

Name ______________________________ Initial Consonant h

Hh

H

hh

h

Print the letter " **h** ".

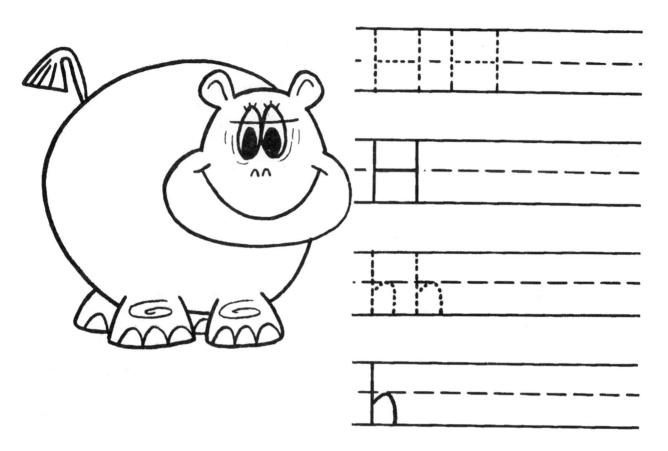

Name ______________________________

Print the letter " **h** ".

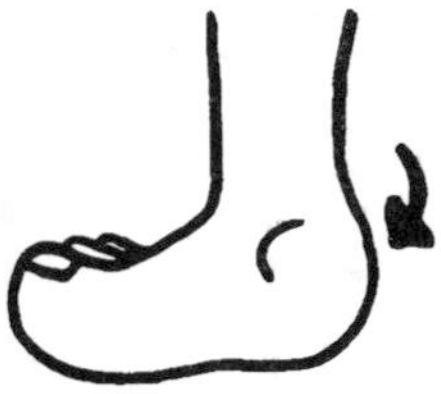

Name ____________________

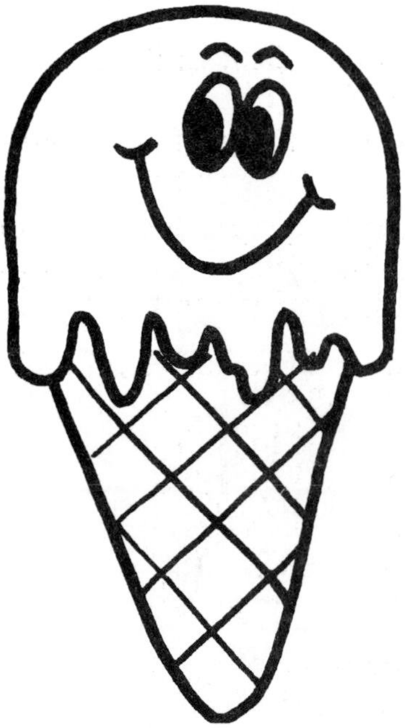

I I

i i

J J

j j

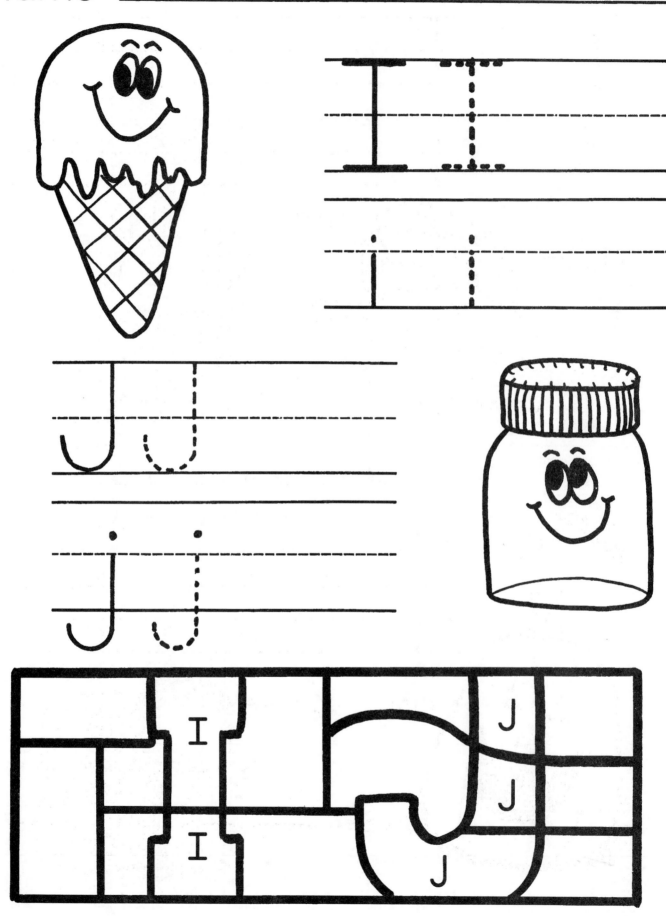

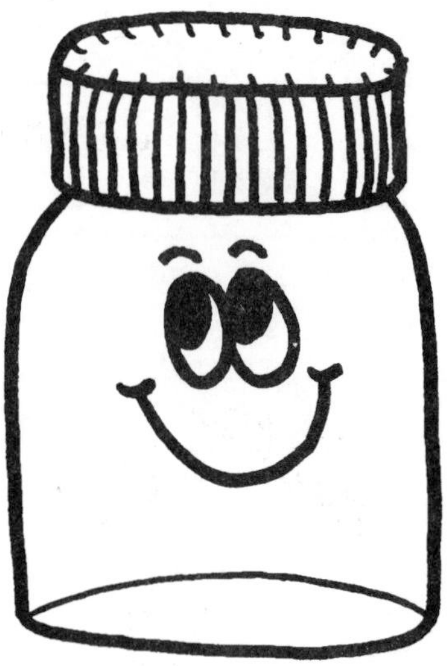

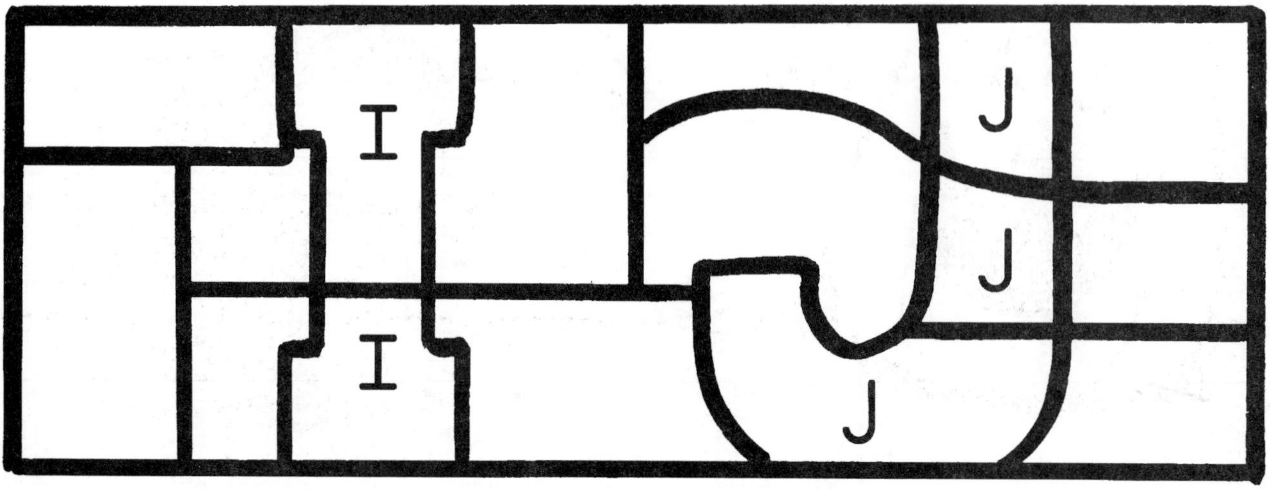

Name ______________________________

I

i

Indian

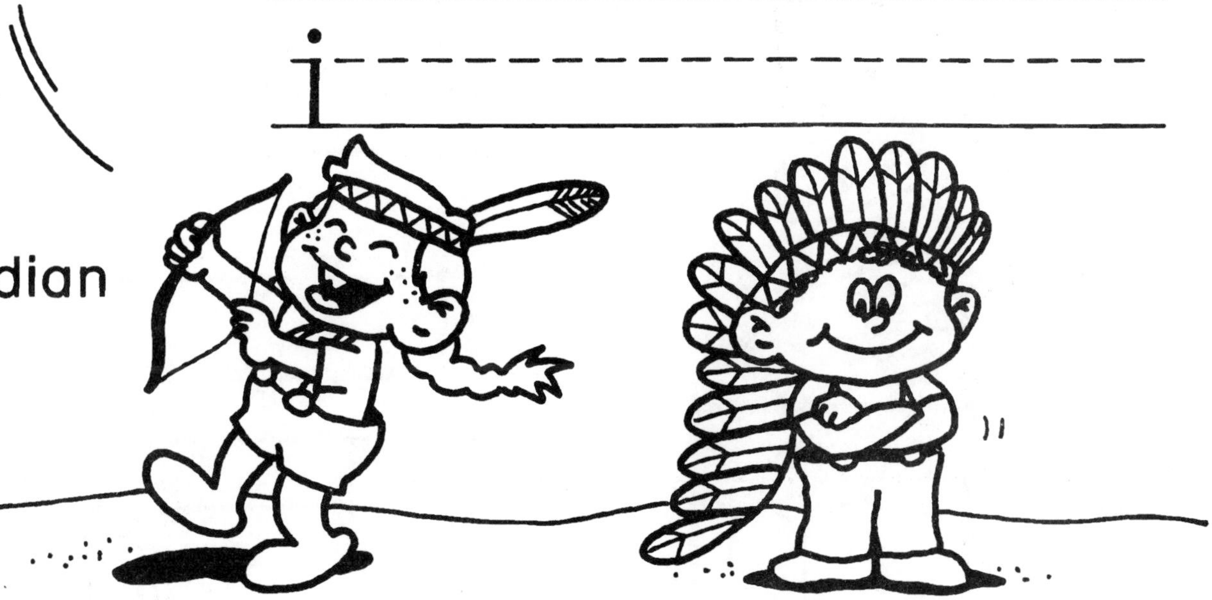

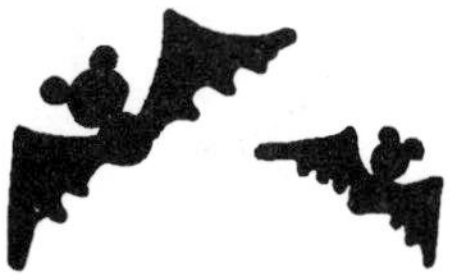

J

j

jack-o'-lantern

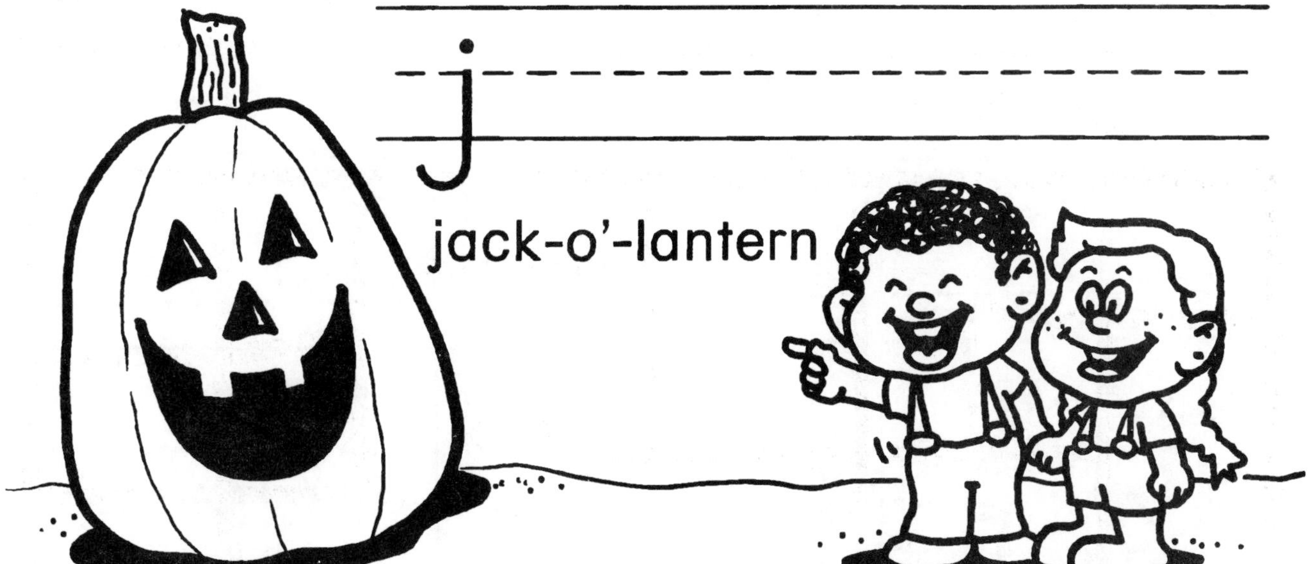

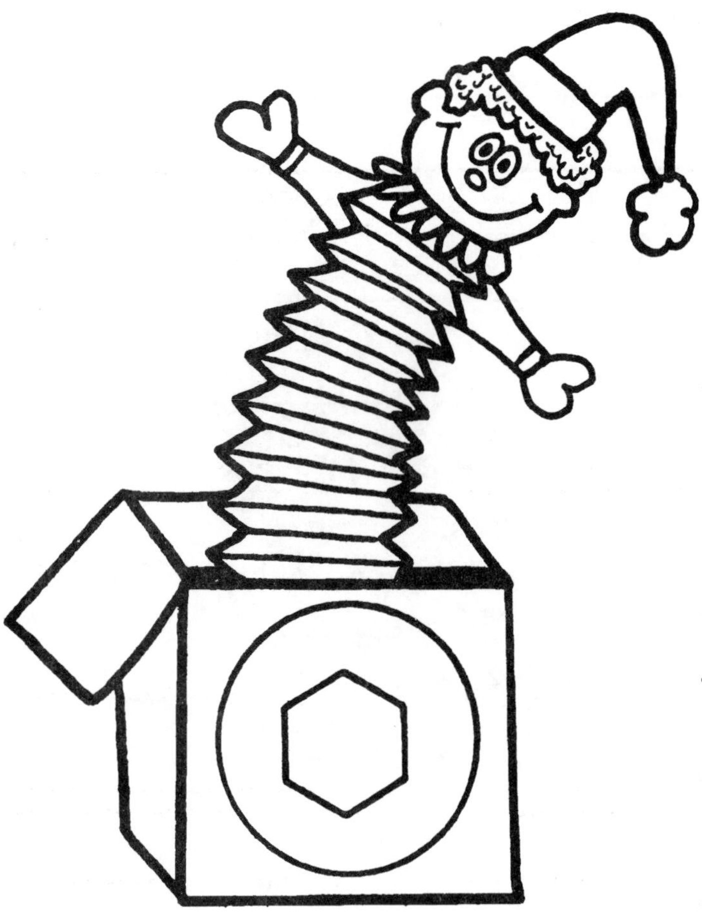

J J

J

j j

j

Print the letter " j ".

Name ____________________

Print the letter " **j** ".

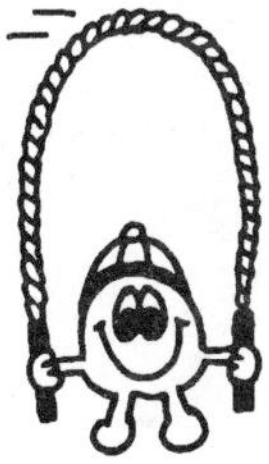

Name ______________________

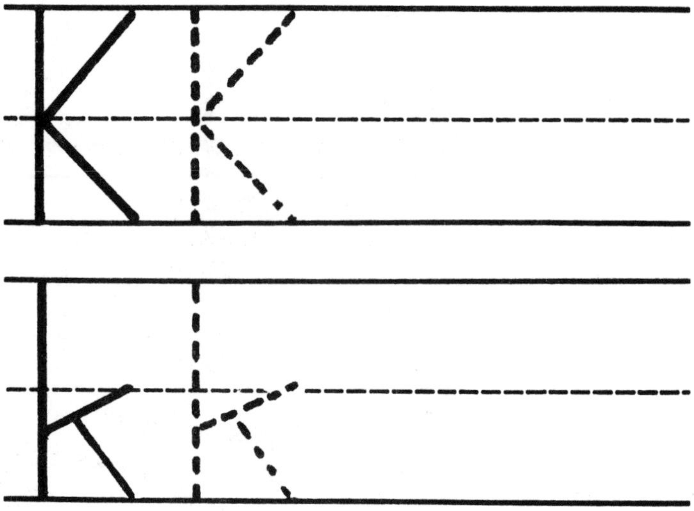

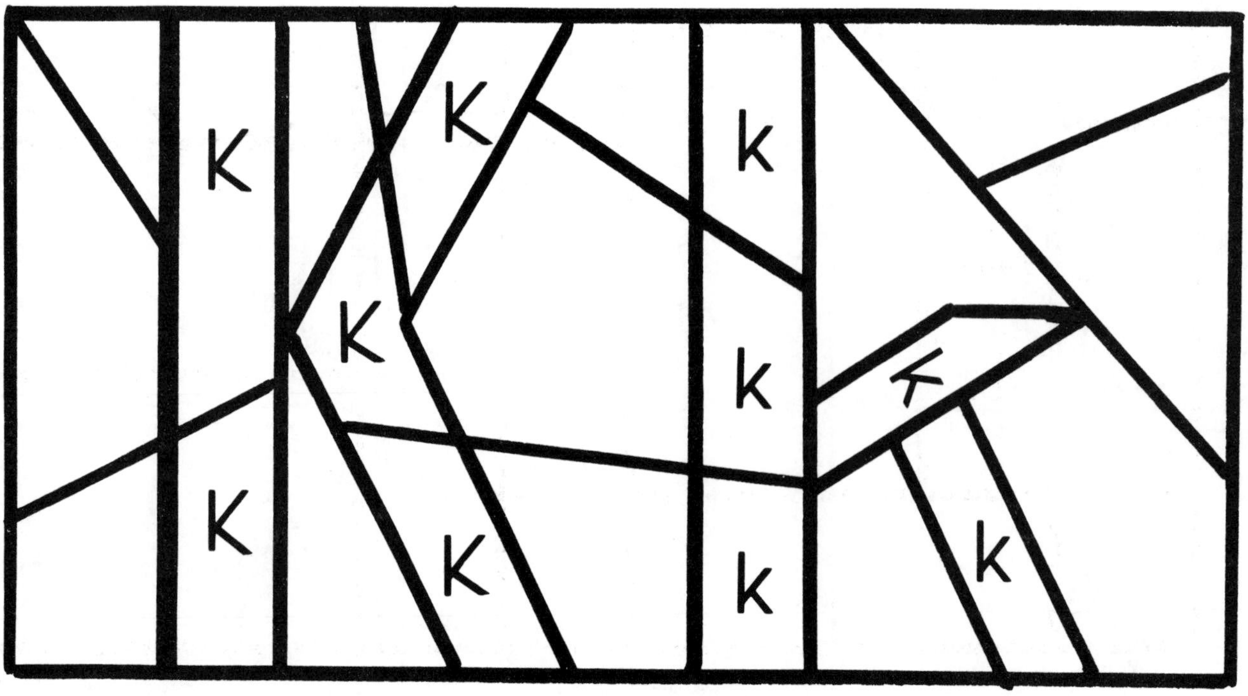

Name ______________________________

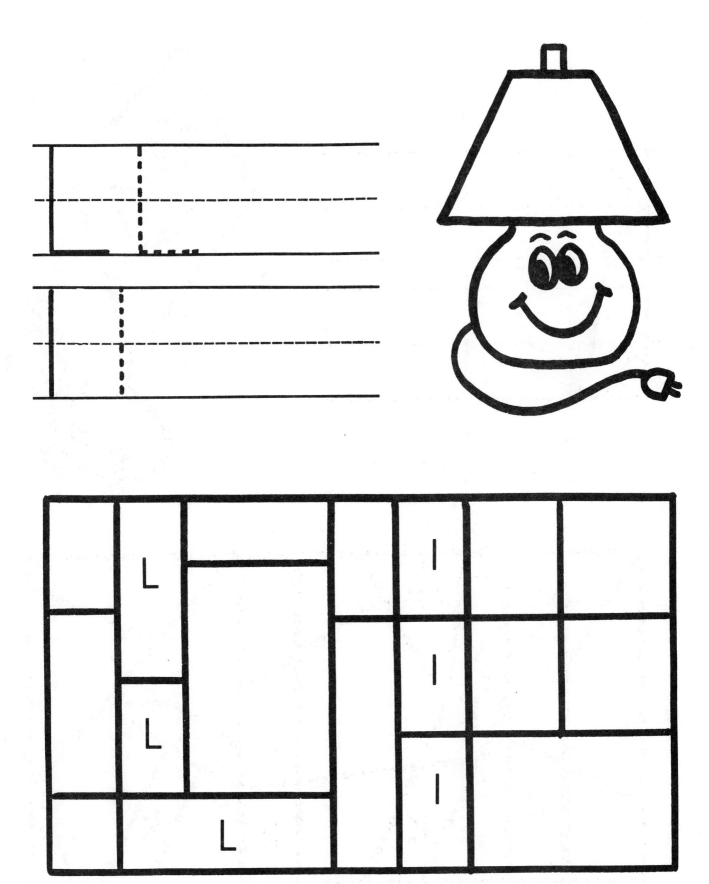

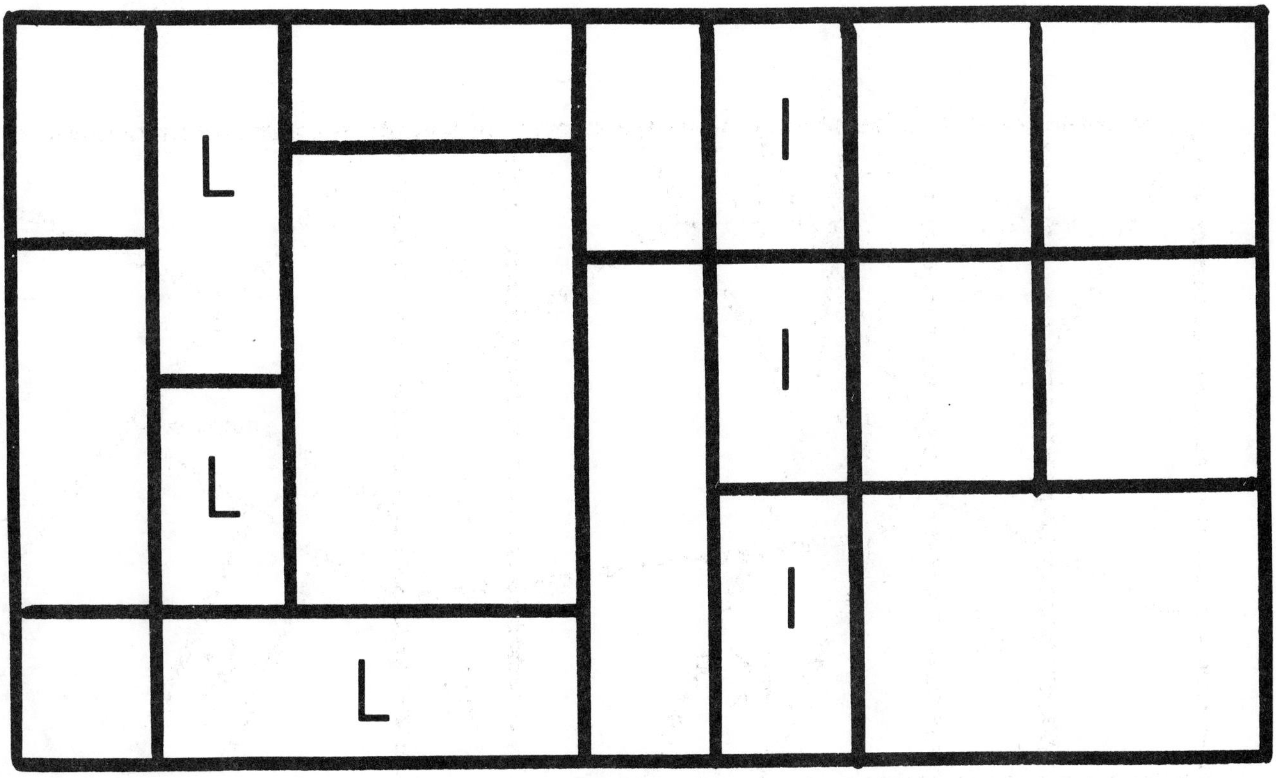

Name ____________________

K

k

koala

L

l

lion

Name

M M

m m

N N

n n

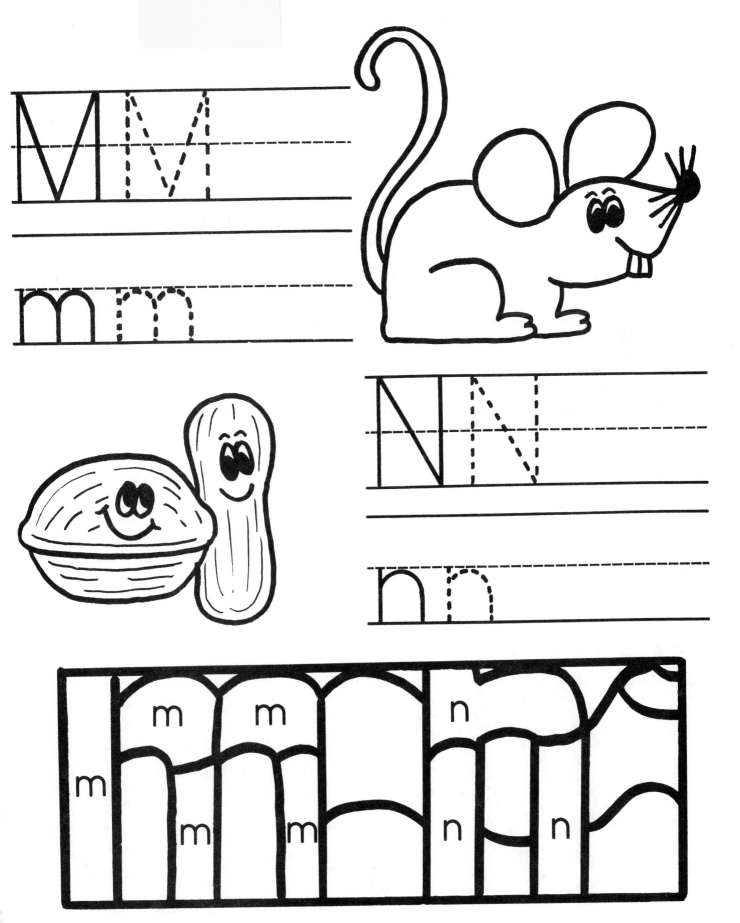

Name ______________________

M

m

mice

N

n

net

Name ______________________________

Draw a line to the letter with the same name.

H	j
I	m
J	i
K	h
L	n
M	l
N	k

Trace and name each letter.

K I J L N H M

k i j l n h m

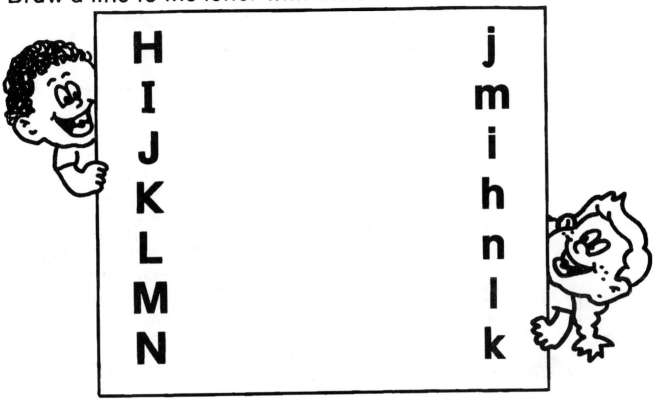

Name

O O

o o

P P

p p

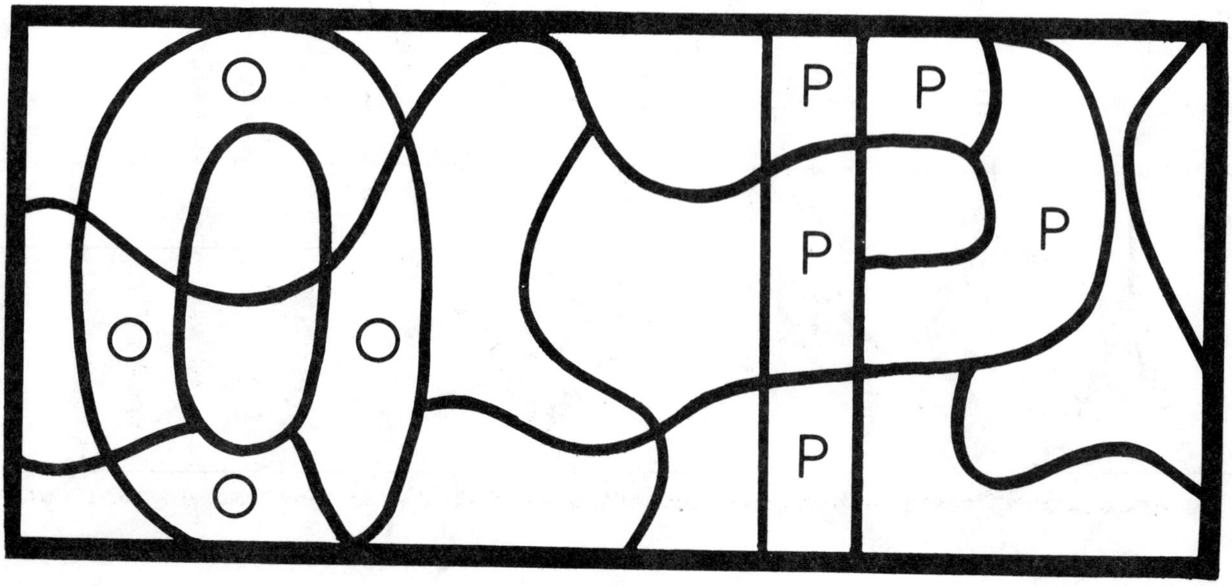

Name ______________________________

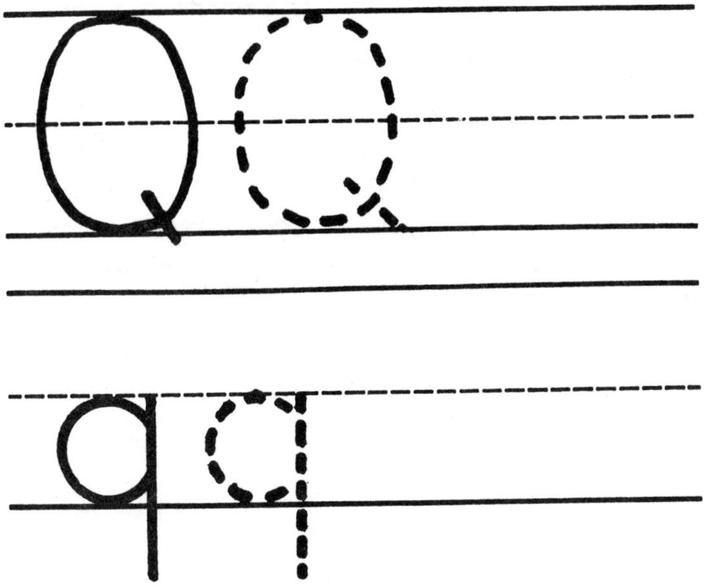

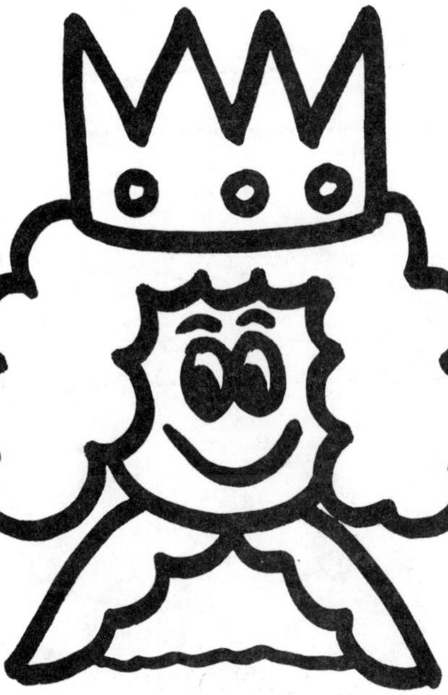

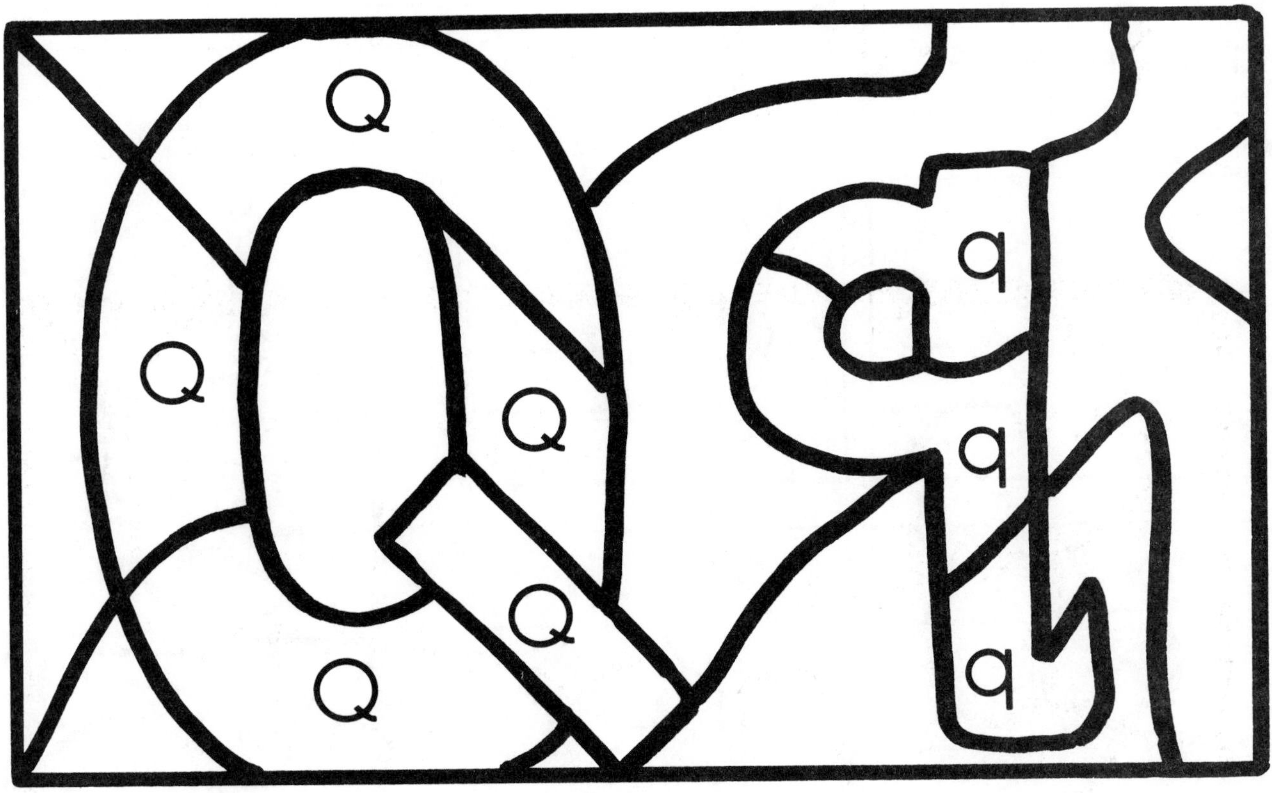

Name ____________________

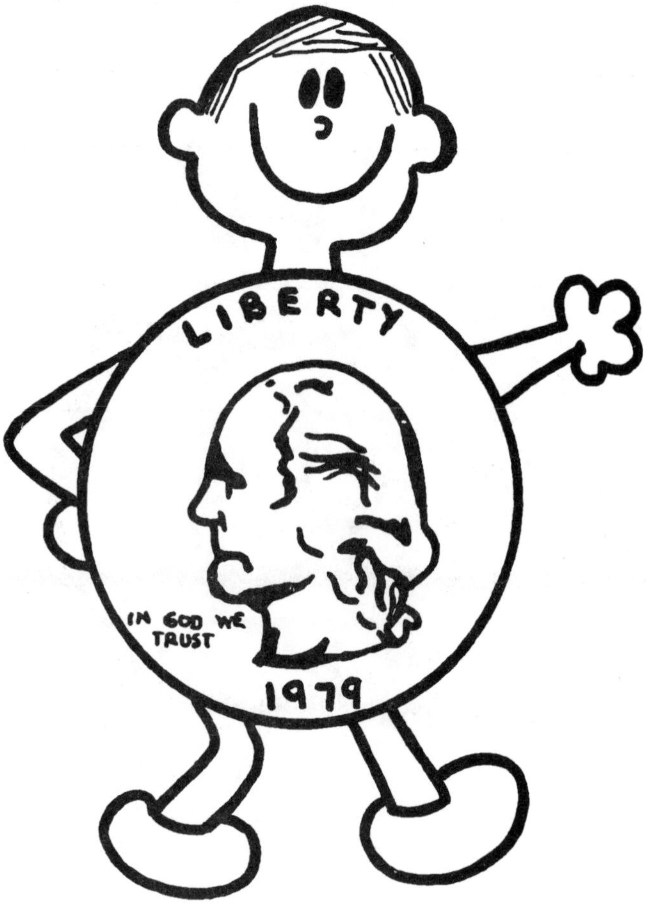

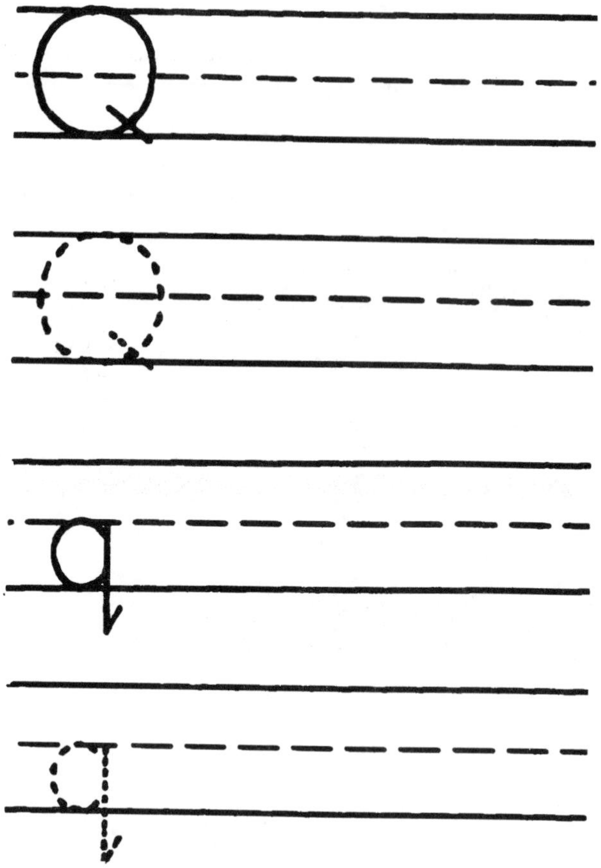

Print the letter " **q** ".

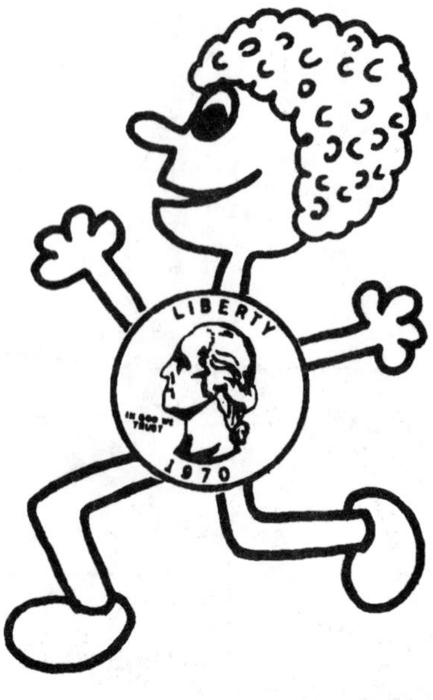

Name

P

p

pig

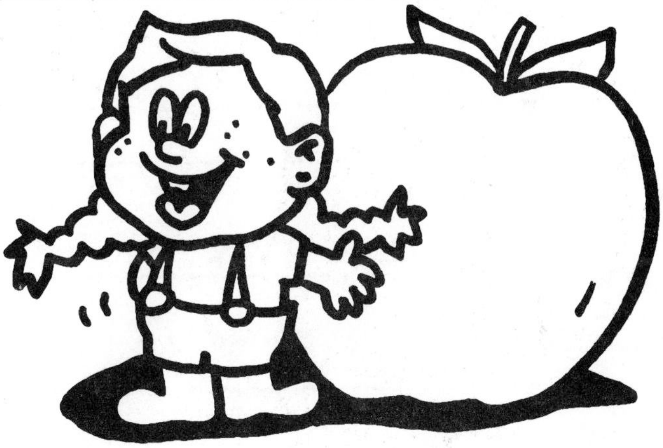

Q

q

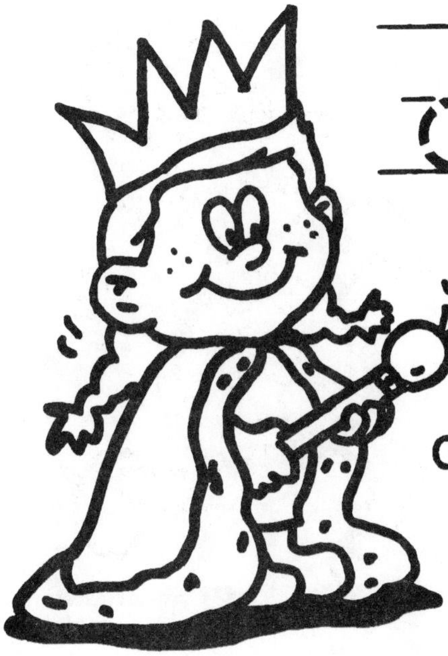

queen

Name ____________________

R R

r r

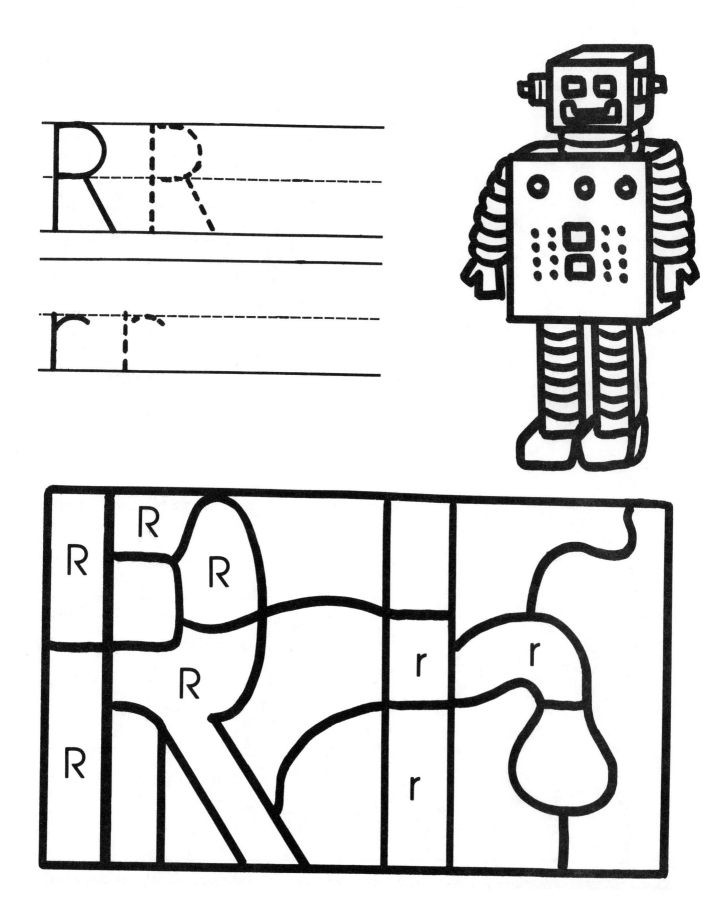

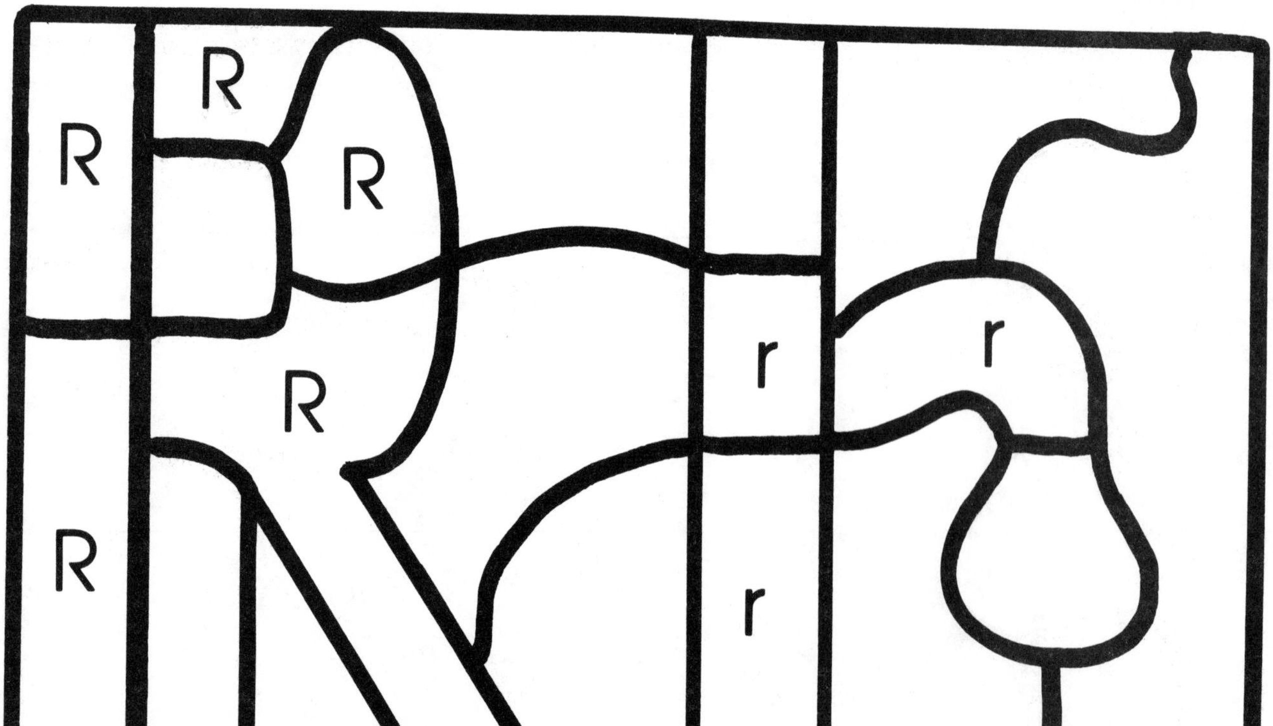

Name ______________________________

S S

s s

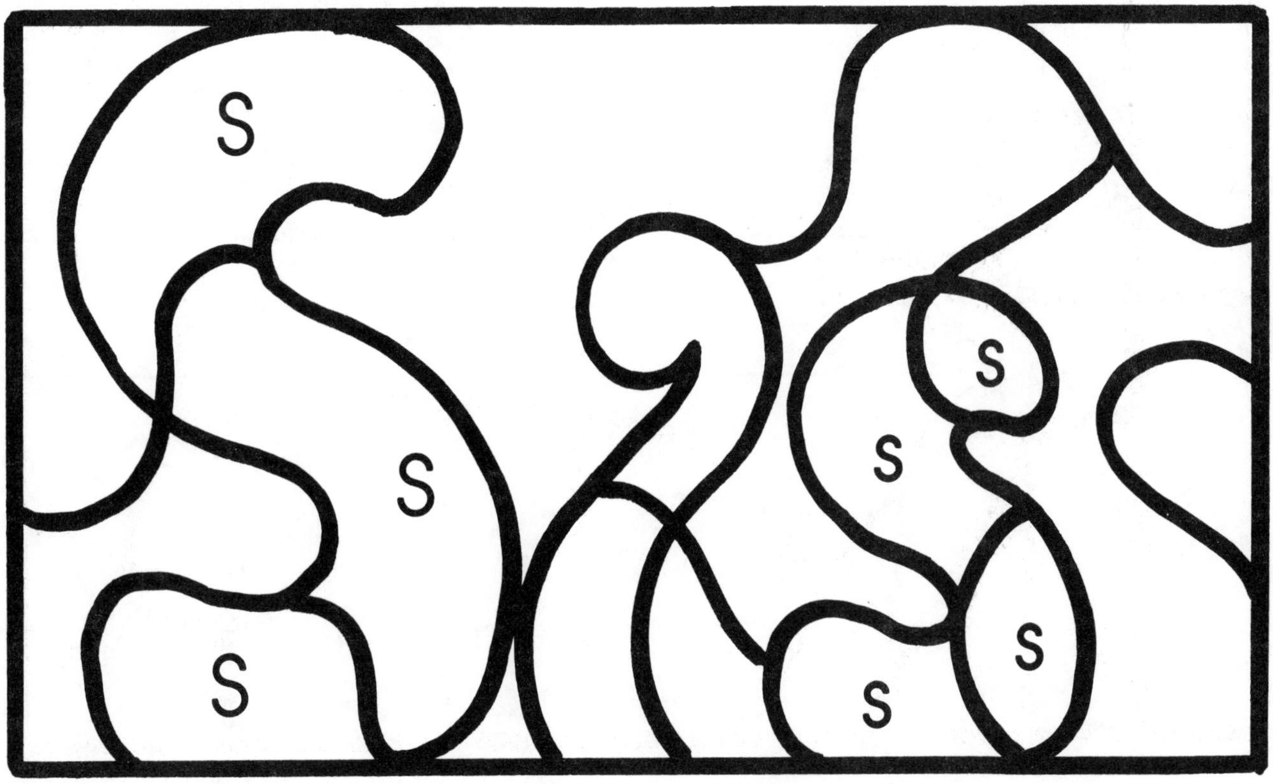

Name ____________________

R

r

rabbit

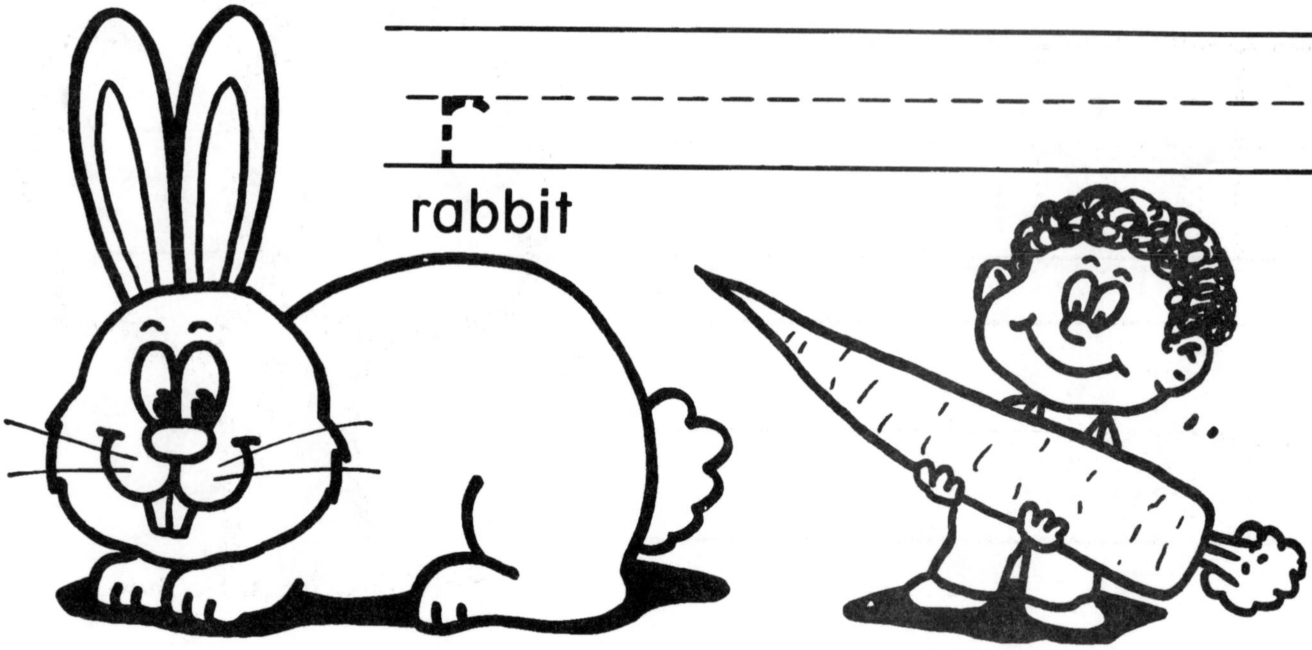

S

s

seal

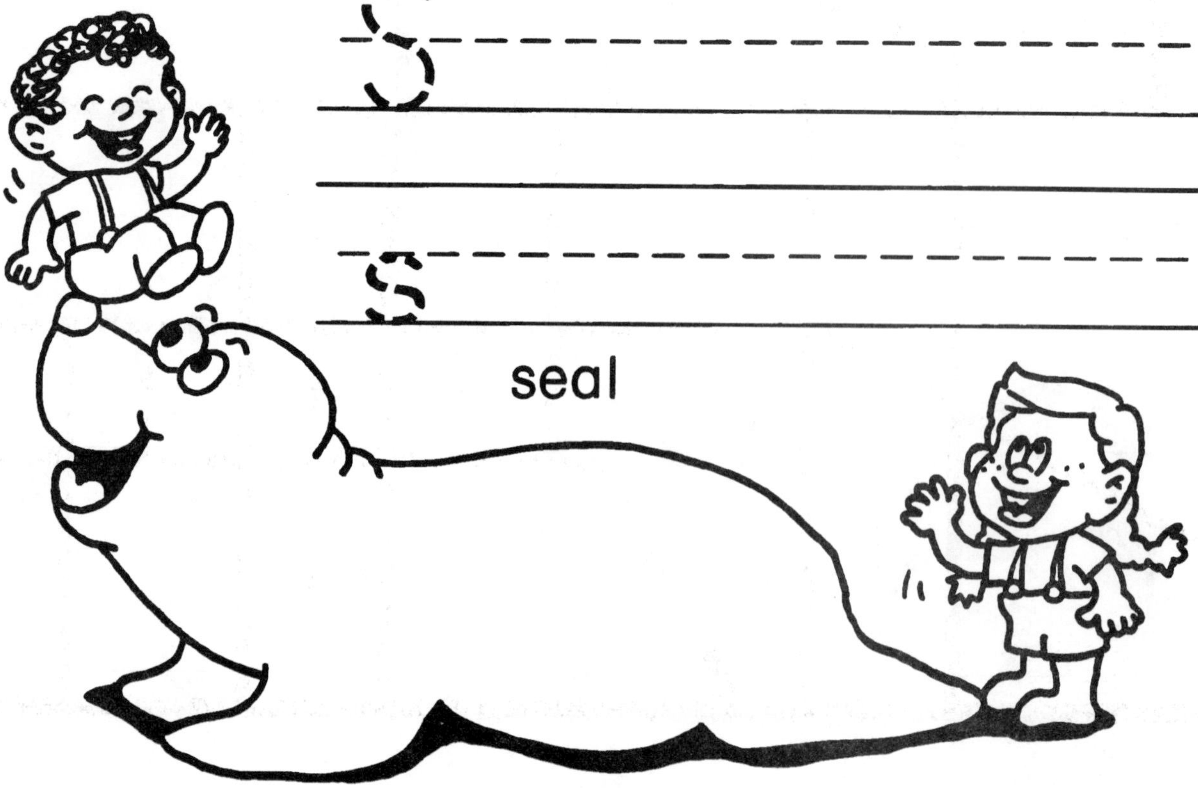

Name ______________________________

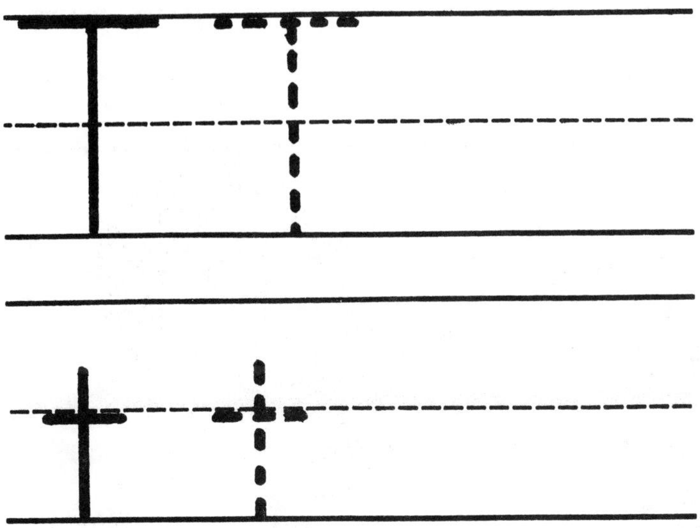

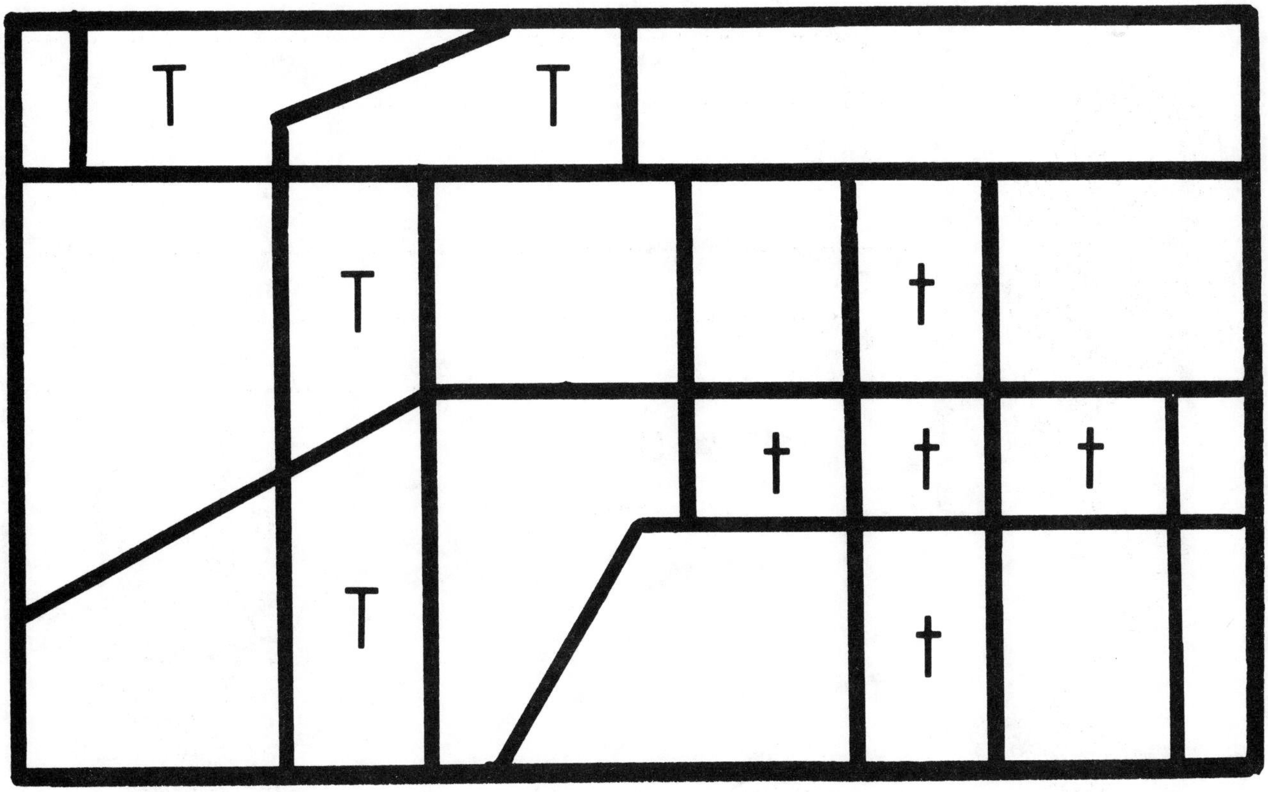

Name ______________________

U U

u u

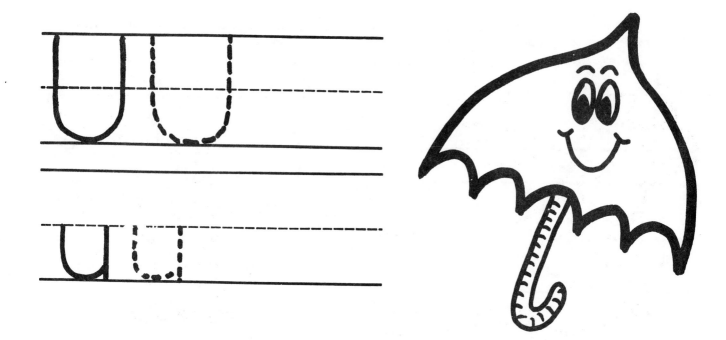

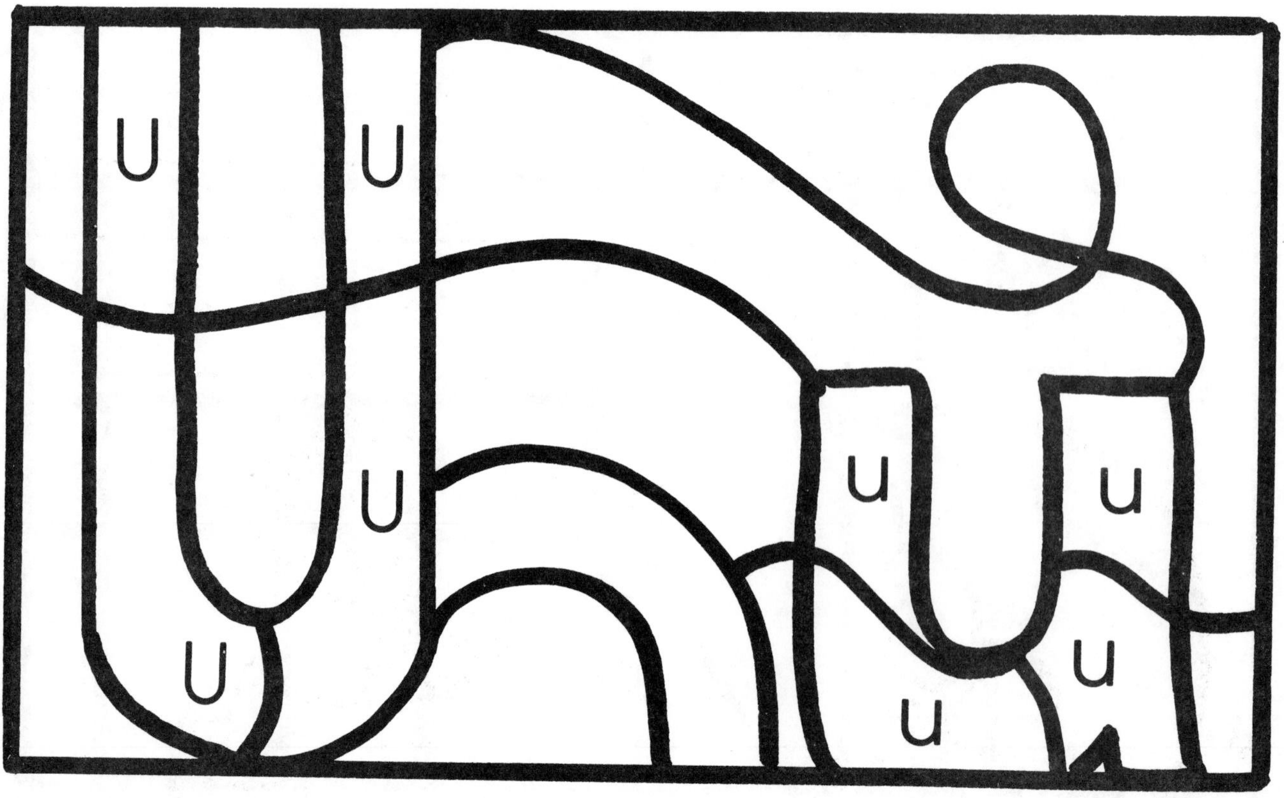

Name ______________________________

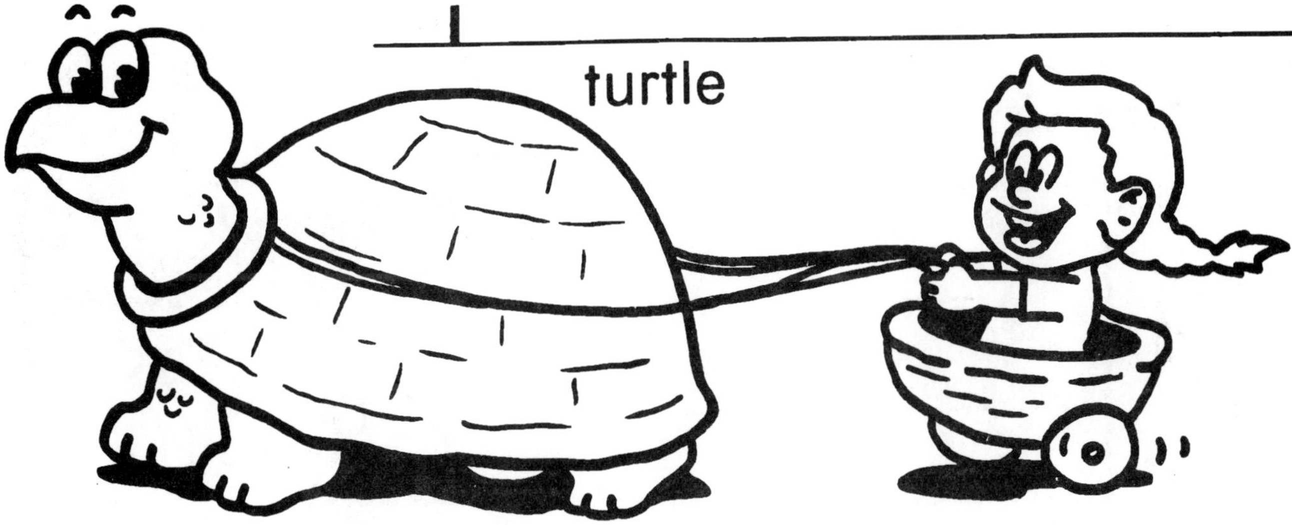

Name ______________________________

Draw a line to the letter with the same name.

O	s
P	u
Q	p
R	r
S	q
T	t
U	o

Trace and name each letter.

U S P Q R O T

u s p q r o t

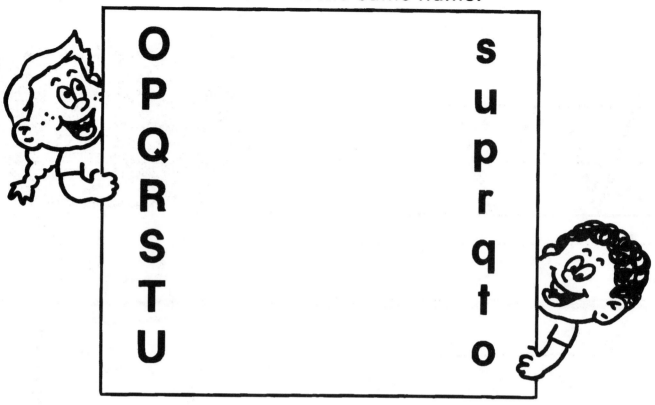

Name ______________________________

V V

v v

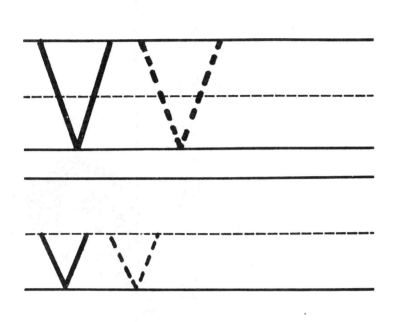

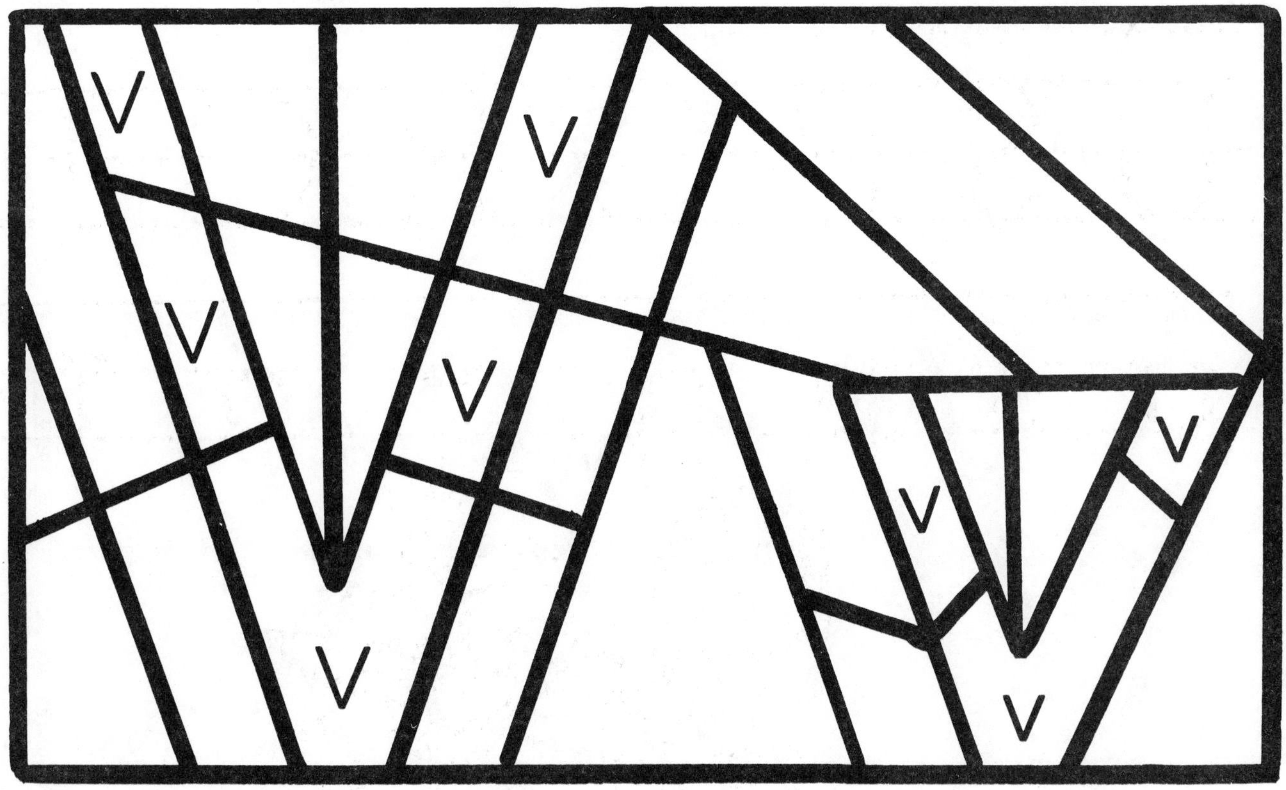

Name ____________________

W W

w w

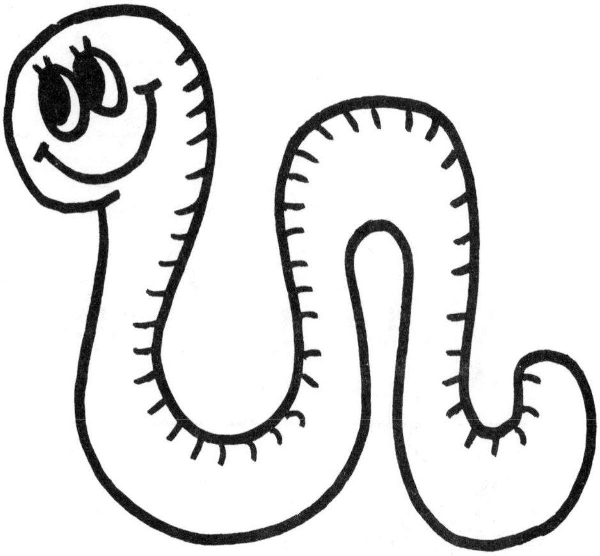

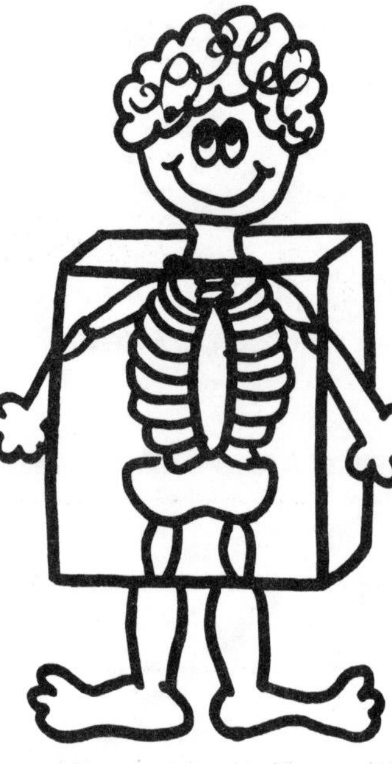

X X

x x

Name ______________________________

W

w

wagon

X

x

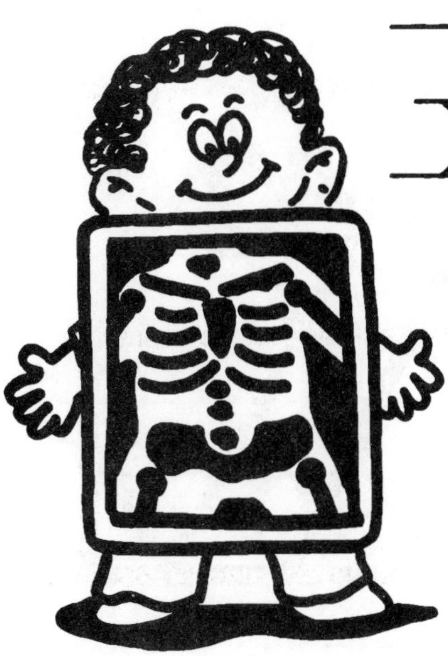

x-ray

Name ______________________ Consonant x

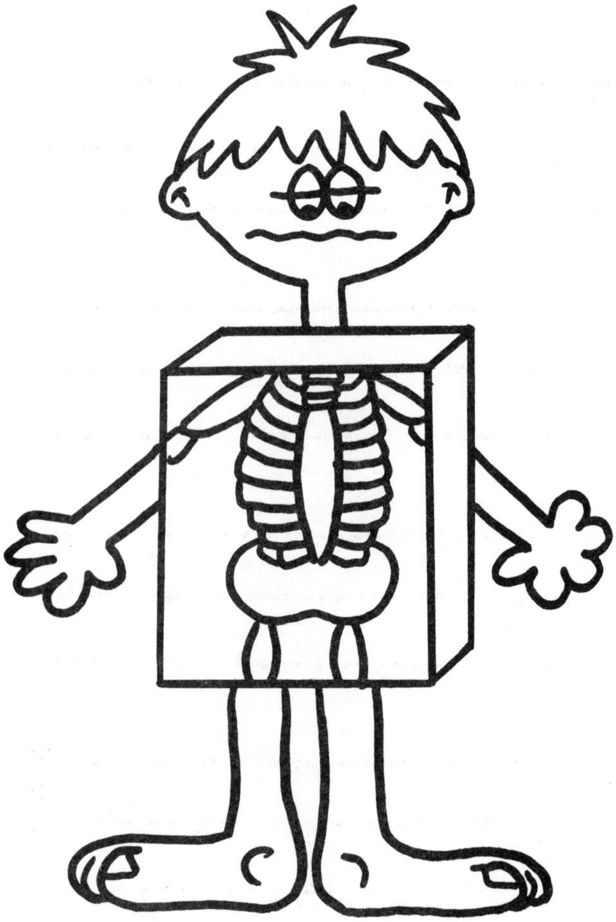

X X

X

x x

x

Color the "**x**" pictures. Trace over the words. The "**x**" is at the beginning or end of the word.

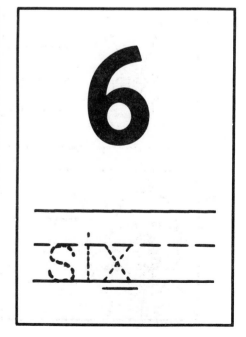

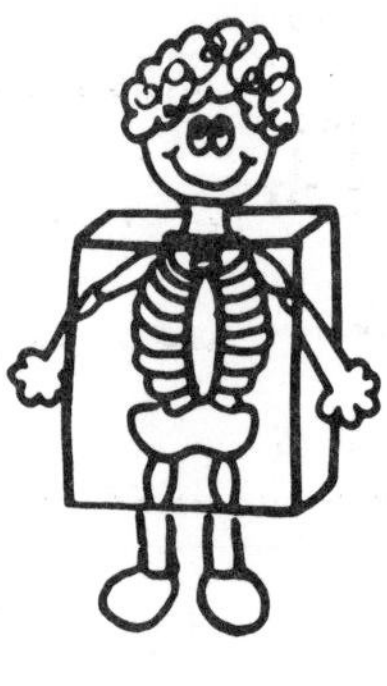	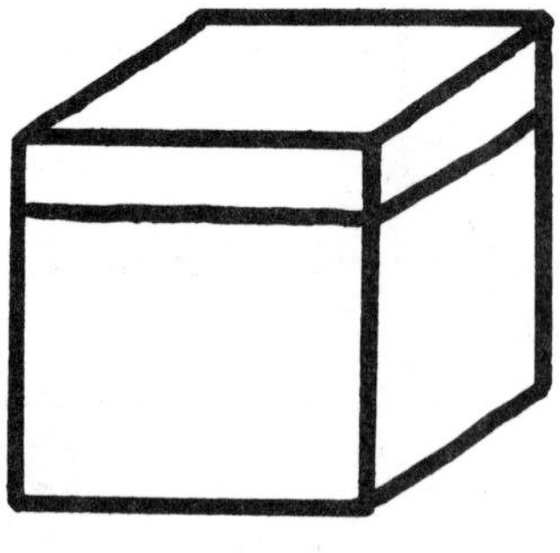	6
x-ray	box	six

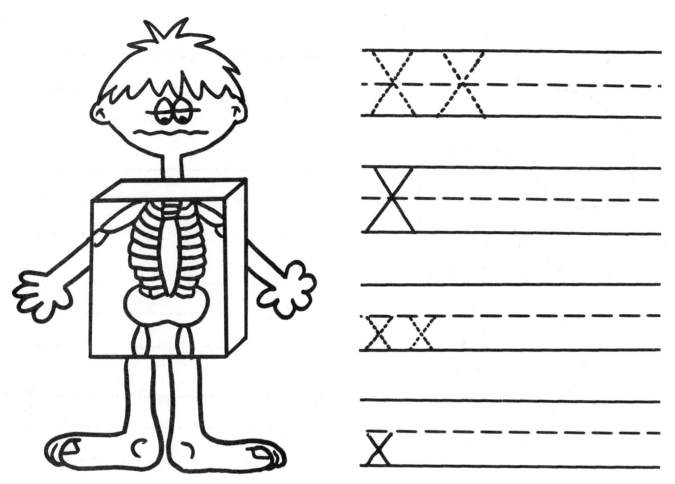

Name ____________________

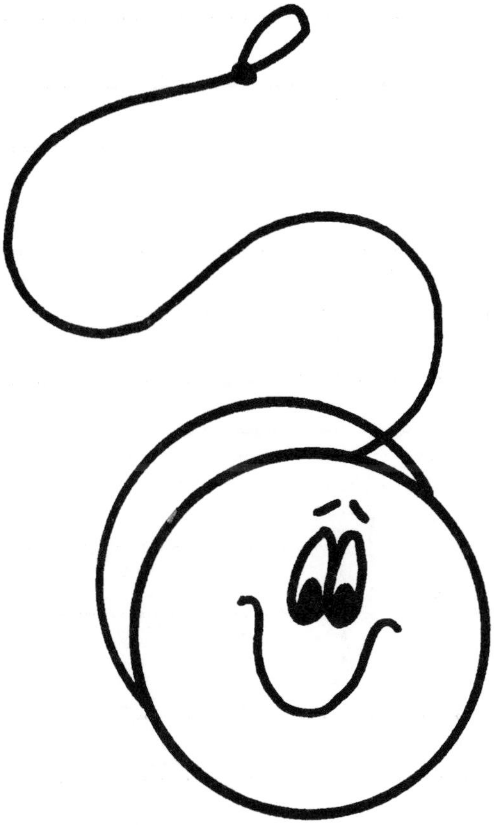

Y

y

Print the letter " **y** ".

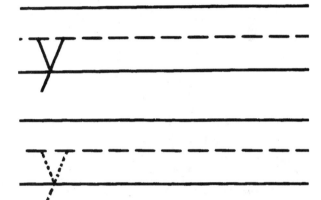

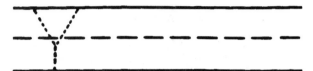

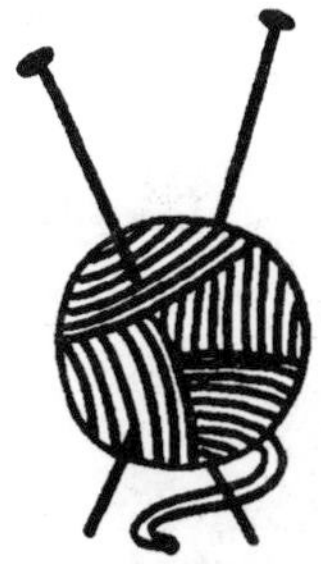

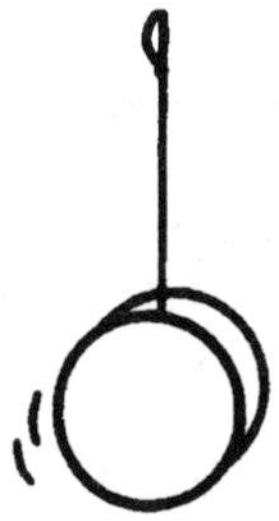

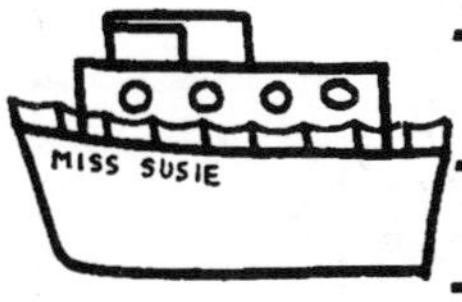

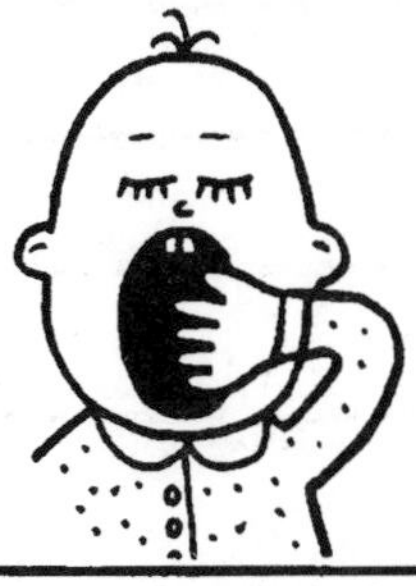

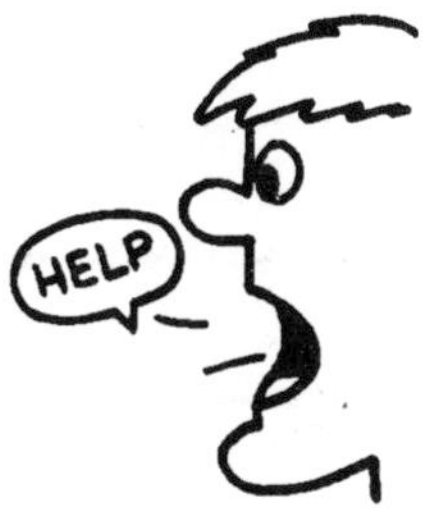

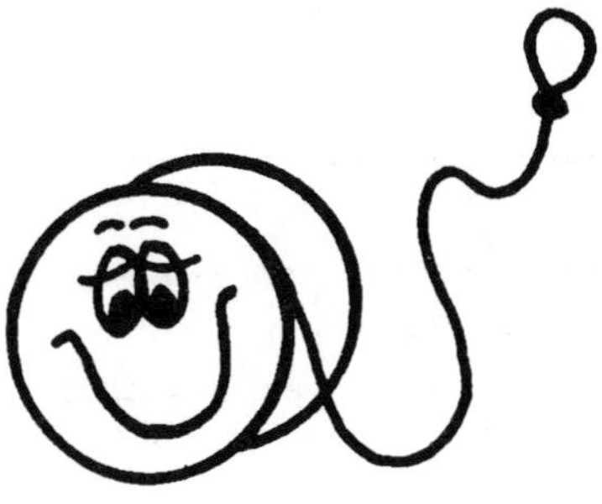

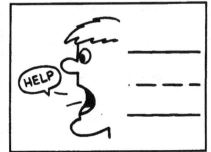

Name ______________________________

Print the letter " **y** ".

Name ________________________________

Y Y

y y

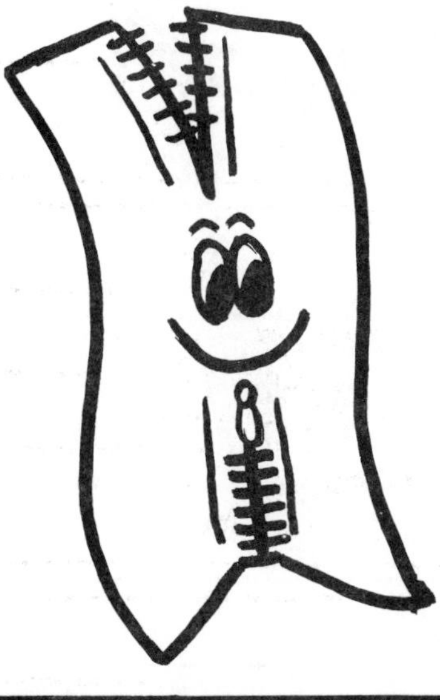

Z Z

z z

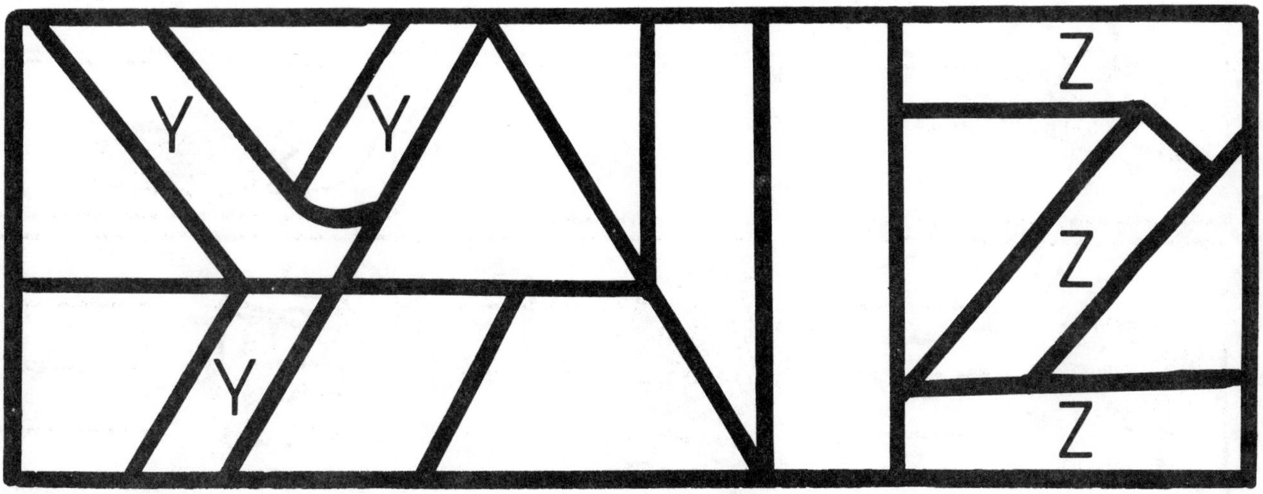

Name

Y

y

Z

z

Name ______________________ Initial Consonant z

Z

z

Print the letter " z ".

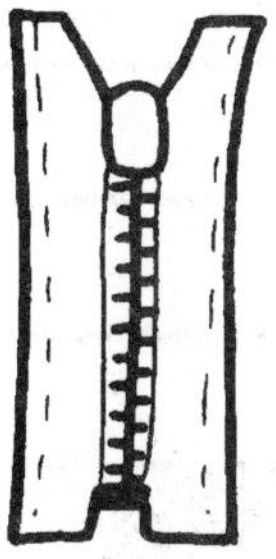

0

Name ________________________________

Draw a line to the letter with the same name.

V	z
W	y
X	x
Y	w
Z	v

Trace and name each letter.

Z X Y W V

z x y w v

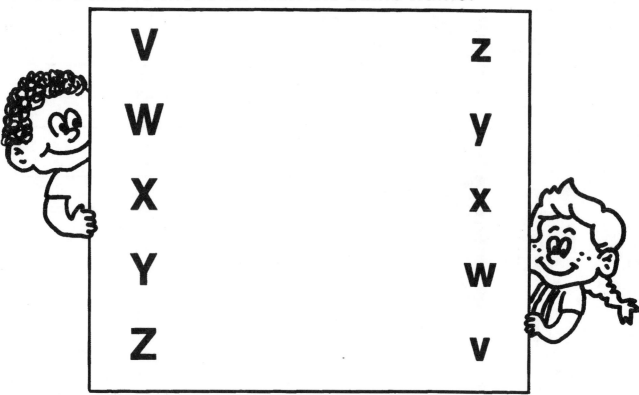